Behind Rebel Lines

ODYSSEY

Behind
Rebel Lines

The Incredible Story of Emma Edmonds, Civil War Spy

SEYMOUR REIT

An Odyssey/Great Episodes Book
Harcourt Brace Jovanovich, Publishers
San Diego   New York   London

Requests for permission to make copies of any part of the work should be
mailed to: Permissions Department, Harcourt Brace Jovanovich, Publishers,
Orlando, Florida 32887.

Library of Congress Cataloging-in-Publication Data
Reit, Seymour.
Behind rebel lines: the incredible story of Emma Edmonds,
Civil War spy/Seymour Reit.
p.   cm.
"An Odyssey book."
Summary: Recounts the story of the Canadian woman who disguised
herself as a man and slipped behind Confederate lines
to spy for the Union army.
ISBN 0-15-200424-6
1. Edmonds, S. Emma E. (Sarah Emma Evelyn), 1841–1898 — Juvenile
literature. 2. United States — History — Civil War, 1861–1865 Secret
service — Juvenile literature. 3. Spies — United States — Biography—
Juvenile literature. [1. Edmonds, S. Emma E. (Sarah Emma Evelyn),
1841–1898. 2. Spies. 3. United States — History — Civil War,
1861–1865 — Secret service.] I. Title.
E608.E235R45   1991
973.7'85'092 — dc20
[B]   [92]   90-45524

Printed in the United States of America

A B C D E

To my colleagues and friends
of the
Bank Street College Media Group

I am naturally fond of adventure,
a little ambitious, and a good deal
romantic—but patriotism was the true
secret of my success.
　　　—from Emma's memoirs

To Begin

This is the true story of a remarkable woman named Emma Edmonds (her full name was really Sarah Emma Edmonds, but she dropped the Sarah part early on in her life). Emma was a feminist long before the word became popular. In 1861, at the start of the Civil War, she joined the Union army disguised as a man and was in the thick of the battle for several years.

Emma Edmonds wasn't the only woman to attempt this. Historians estimate that over *four hundred* women, on both sides, fought in the war posing as men! Wearing men's uniforms, they proved as valiant as any of the soldiers. For pure excitement and suspense, however, Emma's wild adventures are in a class by themselves.

Some of the events described in these pages come from her own memoirs, published after the war. Other facts are from U.S. Army records and

National Archives files. And some material is from the writings of such eminent historians as Bruce Catton, Sylvia Dannett, Mary E. Massey, and Philip Van Doren Stern.

Bits and pieces of this unique tale have appeared in various places, but this is the first time the whole amazing war drama has been set down. Everything that follows is true. All the dates and places are accurate. All the people were real. And all these things actually happened to young Canadian-born Emma Edmonds.

Of course, to make the past come truly alive, the people must come alive—they must be human and believable. For this reason, certain liberties have been taken: some speeches, thoughts, and minor events have been filled in "as they could have been." But this has been done only where necessary, with great care and respect for Emma and her work.

Emma Edmonds was a true idealist. She believed deeply in the Northern cause and reacted to those heroic years with great passion. During the war, Oliver Wendell Holmes, Jr., who became a famous Supreme Court justice, was a young officer in the Union forces. Years later, he wrote: "Through our great good fortune, in our youth our hearts were touched with fire."

So it was with Emma Edmonds—and here is her story.

1

April 25, 1861

The long line stretched from the Flint courthouse down the stone steps and across the green lawn. Moving forward slowly, the young men were in high spirits. They laughed and joked as if they were leaving on a picnic instead of going off to fight a war.

"I'll wager we take Richmond in three weeks."

"Southerners talk big, but they cain't fight."

"Been plowin' behind horses all my life. Now I'll get me a chance to ride one."

"Can't hardly wait to take a shot at a live rebel."

"You may be too late, boy. They say one good battle, the Confederacy'll fall apart."

Tension and excitement crackled along the noisy line. But one dark-haired volunteer, small and silent, was lost in thought. Emma Edmonds tugged at her jacket and prayed—for the tenth time that day—that the scheme would work. It was plumb crazy, she knew, but she didn't care. She'd made up her mind and that was that.

Would they discover her secret? She'd have her answer in a few minutes. Of course, she was comfortable enough wearing men's clothes. She'd practically lived in rough pants and heavy shoes growing up in Canada, working with the farmhands, and keeping up with the best of them. Now at twenty-one, she was still trim and boyish. She had a strong chin, a firm mouth, and cool blue eyes, and she'd cropped her hair short like a man's.

She also knew—she'd checked earlier—that nobody bothered with physical examinations for new recruits. The Union army was desperate for able-bodied men; they had no mind to be choosy. Still she was worried. Maybe her information was wrong. Maybe they'd see right through her masquerade.

The line inched slowly along step by step, carrying Emma past a billboard covered with recruiting posters. The words leapt out at her: Volunteers to the RESCUE! . . . PATRIOTISM and LOVE of COUNTRY! . . . Ruthless Southern TREACHERY! . . . DEFEND our NOBLE UNION! . . . VINDICATE the HONOR of our GLORIOUS FLAG!

She frowned at the fancy wording—all that fuss and bombast. Still, she had to admit that was how she really felt—she and thousands of others. Bother the fancy speeches and flag-waving politicians—the fact was that alarm bells were ringing everywhere. The country was in peril and had to be saved.

Only ten days before, Abe Lincoln had asked for seventy-five thousand volunteers. Now they were pouring in from shops and factories, mills and mines, offices, farms, and dockyards—rallying in every city, town, and village. And so were the local militias, with their fancy names and uniforms. Emma had read in the papers about Ellsworth's Avengers, Smallwood's Marylanders, Sprague's Light Cavalry; she knew of the Black Rifles, the Winslow Blues, and the Hibernian Greens. She'd seen pictures of New York's Fire Zouaves who wore baggy red pantaloons. The Putnam Phalanx of Connecticut sported white plumes on their hats. Boston's Highland Guards had uniforms of Scotch plaid. And one group, the Mozart Regiment, had marched off to battle in elegant double-breasted frock coats. But that was changing; all these units, so nobly costumed, were now being welded into a single force wearing Federal blue.

Here in Flint, where Emma lived, men were needed for the Michigan Volunteer Infantry called the Union Grays. Emma was aching to be a nurse in a tent hospital on the battlefield, but that was dangerous work: only male nurses were given those jobs.

The line carried Emma to the foot of the court-house steps. She climbed them slowly, her heart hammering. With each step, her anxiety grew.

Certainly there were things she could do as a woman to help out. She could knit socks, roll bandages, or sew flags for the new regiments. She could work in a New England textile mill, making cloth for blankets and uniforms. Or fill cartridge sacks with gunpowder at a Federal arsenal. Or work in a refreshment canteen. Or write letters home for the sick and wounded. Female nurses were also needed at hospitals in big cities like Philadelphia, Boston, and New York.

It was all good work, important work—useful work that would trap her on the sidelines, far away from the realities of the war. But safety wasn't for Emma Edmonds. Something was driving her to do more, to play a bigger part. There was a kind of imp voice inside her, pushing her to take risks. It was the same voice that, years before, had dared her to climb the highest trees on the farm, to ride the most dangerous horses, to swim the river raging wild after the spring floods.

Emma couldn't put this feeling into words, but she sensed that at least part of it was her father's doing. He had always wanted a son and could never forgive her for being female. She'd tried hard to please him and to win his approval, but without success. Her father had acted as though the whole thing were *her* fault, and his hard manner never softened. After Emma's mother died, his criticism and cruel tirades got worse, and when Emma was sixteen, she ran for her life. Taking all she owned in an old burlap sack, she fled to a country where she knew words like *liberty* and *freedom* had real meaning.

That had been five years ago, and Emma had quickly fallen in love with her adopted land. She'd become its strong defender, and now that America was in peril she'd have to take action. The imp voice was calling her. Somehow she *had* to be part of this war. She *had* to be right there with the fighting men. Emma, unafraid, sharing their dangers and hardships. . . .

Suddenly, she found herself in a paneled room draped with American flags. The line had carried her with it through the tall doors, and now her turn had come. With a final tug at her jacket, Emma swallowed hard and stepped to the desk. The recruiting sergeant glanced quickly at her and bent over his paper.

"Name and age?" he asked mechanically.

"Franklin Thompson," said Emma. "Twenty-one."

"Place of birth?"

"St. John, Canada."

The sergeant looked at Emma again, but only for a moment. In this area many Canadians were crossing the border to join the Federal army. He nodded and went on.

"Any handicaps or infectious diseases?"

"No, sir."

"Civil occupation?"

"Bible salesman and medical orderly. I'm hoping I can be posted to a field hospital."

"Read and write?"

"Yes, sir."

He pushed the enlistment form over for her to sign. Taking the pen, Emma dipped it, remembering just in time to scrawl *Franklin Thompson*.

The soldier scribbled on a card, handed it to her, and jerked a thumb over his shoulder. "We're short of medical help so I'm rating you as a field nurse. Report to the supply tent for your gear and get sworn in."

The huge supply tent, pitched near the courthouse, was chaotic, but somehow everything worked efficiently. Moving from line to line, Emma collected a blanket, boots, tin canteen, and army clothing. Then, with scores of others, she raised her hand and took the oath of service, administered by an elderly, tired-looking adjutant.

"You men," he said, "are now part of the Second Regiment, Michigan Volunteers. Report to the railway depot tomorrow at 5:00 A.M. sharp. You'll go by train to Washington, where the regiment will be issued weapons and become part of the Army of the Potomac. Good luck to you all."

Emma felt a great surge of relief at passing the big test. Carrying her equipment, she slipped away from the excited crowd and hurried across the trampled lawn. The line was still growing; it seemed like every young man in the state was rushing to enlist.

Back at the rooming house she dumped everything on her bed and carefully locked the door. Forcing herself to stay calm, she began the magic change. Trousers . . . shirt . . . jacket and boots . . . peaked cap . . . wide belt with the U.S. brass buckle . . . canvas leggings . . . rolled blanket over the shoulder, just so. Then in the cracked mirror over her bureau, she sized herself up, studying her reflection from different angles. Convincing, no doubt about it. Emma Edmonds was gone, and in her place stood Pvt. Franklin Thompson, Second Michigan Volunteers, U.S. Army!

Marching around the little room, getting used to the new uniform, Emma felt more comfortable and sure of herself. Her masquerade, starting as an impulsive, daft sort of idea, had suddenly become real.

Outside her window a party of young recruits tramped by, their arms loaded with gear, their voices raised in harmony:

> *We will welcome to our ranks*
> *All the loyal, true and brave,*
> *Shouting the battle cry of Freedom;*
> *And altho' they may be poor,*
> *Not a man shall be a slave,*
> *Shouting the battle cry of Freedom!*

Emma tried to join in, but her mouth was dry. Her heart pounded and she felt light-headed. Was it joy or fear? She couldn't rightly say—odd how both these emotions had symptoms in common. But no matter—the important thing was that her scheme had worked. So far, she was safe.

Emma stared in the mirror again, tilted her cap at a jaunty, devil-may-care angle, and smiled, wondering what her father would say if he could see her now. She felt a great rush of excitement and happiness. The imp voice had pulled her from the sidelines and the adventure was beginning. Of course there would be problems—there were bound to be—but she wasn't worried. At least, not too much. Whatever trouble or dangers might be waiting, Emma knew somehow she'd manage to face them.

Standing at the window, she could still hear the volunteers singing in the distance. She drew a long, slow breath. This morning she'd taken a soldier's solemn oath; now there was no turning back. For better or worse, Miss Edmonds was going to war.

2

March 19, 1862

Pvt. Thompson was dog tired. He gulped some luke-warm water from his canteen, picked up his musket, and headed wearily toward the hospital tent. His eyes burned. His shoulders ached. The sergeant's harsh voice rang in his ears.

"Dress those lines! Quick march! Try to look like soldiers!"

"When you crawl, keep your fool heads down! You want to stop a sniper's ball?"

"Thompson, that's a musket you're carrying, not a mop handle!"

Under a blazing Virginia sun, the troopers of the Michigan Second had been bullied and badgered. They marched for hours, learning military drill. They practiced priming and firing their weapons. On skirmish exercises, they crawled through acres of dirt and underbrush. It had been a rough day—only one of many.

The war had been dragging on for months, and the South still hadn't collapsed. In fact, the Confederate troops had proved tough and valiant, winning key battles. Gen. George McClellan, commanding the Army of the Potomac, was anxious to change all that. He'd vowed to whip his militias and green recruits into a good fighting force—and no one was exempted. Along with the surgeons and other nurses, Pvt. Franklin Thompson was classed as a noncombatant; still, everyone had to go through the same training. In war nothing was certain; there was no telling when medical and service troops might have to help fight off a sudden enemy attack.

Heading along the tent rows, Pvt. Thompson picked his way around stacked arms and piles of equipment. Supply wagons rumbled by. Couriers on horseback galloped past him, raising clouds of dust. New men were still pouring in and tents were going up everywhere.

He entered the hospital tent and walked to the far end, where a place had been set aside for the nurses. A canvas curtain separated them from the main ward. The tent had been pitched in a shaded area with good drainage, a little apart from the rest of the camp. A row of cots ran along either side, separated by a center aisle. There were some thirty cots in all, but more could be added when necessary.

In the middle of the tent a large sawhorse table was piled with medicines, books, and hospital records. When necessary, it would also serve as an operating table. Kerosene lamps hung here and there on the tent poles, and toward the back of the tent was an open wing where all the meals were cooked.

Thompson's unit—a small one—was made up of the head surgeon, Dr. Hodes; his assistant, Lt. Reese; four male nurses; two cooks; a wardmaster; and an orderly who chopped wood, hauled water, and did the heavy chores. At the moment, the ward was fairly quiet, since the regiment hadn't yet seen heavy fighting. There were the usual cases of dysentery and some sniper gunshot wounds. One officer had cracked a hip when his horse stumbled and fell on him. A young soldier's foot was crushed when a cannon recoiled before he could leap clear. And a veteran of the Mexican War, who'd ridden with Winfield Scott at Cerro Gordo, was down with a case of pneumonia. Other patients who suffered from assorted burns and minor mishaps were treated and then sent back to their outfits.

The soldier peered into the ward and nodded to the men on duty. He dumped his gear and checked the time. Dr. Hodes's nurses worked in pairs—six hours on and six hours off, around the clock. He had a whole hour before his next shift—time enough for a nap and a bite to eat. Lying on the cot with its thin straw mattress, Thompson stretched luxuriously. The sounds of camp life faded away. A few fat flies droned lazily. He closed his eyes and tried to recall all that had happened since "Franklin Thompson" had enlisted.

Of course, those first few weeks had been the roughest. Emma smiled as she thought of how nervous she'd been—how worried that someone would discover her secret. And Lord, what a peck of problems she'd had to face: how to steal a bit of privacy when she needed it, or how to behave around some of the coarser men. Emma was modest by nature but tough and determined. With faith and good humor she'd worked to solve those difficulties, and now Pvt. Thompson was well established with nobody any the wiser.

Stretched out on the cot, Emma relieved her first day in uniform—the long train ride from Flint to Washington, D.C., in a grimy coach crammed with recruits. Unsure of her disguise, she'd kept to herself, gazing out the window and answering curtly if a question came her way.

In Washington, the new men were issued arms and divided into regimental companies. Later Emma had time to explore the bustling capital. There were army uniforms everywhere. Tents and bivouacs were jammed into every inch of park and vacant lot. Space in the city was so scarce that troops were even camped in the big East Room of the White House.

Emma could almost taste the excitement in the air. Knots of civilians gathered around the bulletin boards to read war dispatches. Smart cavalry units trotted down the boulevards, their guidons snapping in the breeze. Fife and drum corps stepped along, piping patriotic tunes. On every wide street, troops practiced marching and drilling. Whenever a company tramped past the big house on Pennsylvania Avenue the men set up a cheer—and sometimes President Lincoln would come to the window and wave.

From her temporary camp, Emma could look straight down Constitution Avenue to the new capitol building still under construction. The huge iron dome was only half finished. Its bare ribs poked up in the air like giant fingers, a vague promise waiting to be fulfilled.

Emma stayed in Washington for months, nursing at a nearby clinic. Then, one day, thousands of troops, including her company, were jammed aboard paddle-wheel transports and carried down Chesapeake Bay. After a slow, bumpy trip, the boats anchored near Fort Monroe at the tip of the Virginia peninsula. The Army of the Potomac, numbering almost one hundred thousand men, took up positions across this neck of land, between the York River and the James River. Emma's regiment was part of the Union line. She'd been assigned to Company F, and was now settled at Dr. Hodes's tent hospital.

McClellan's plan, widely known, was to move north and attack Richmond, the capital of the Confederacy. But the Union's path was blocked by the city of Yorktown, a short way up the peninsula. This city was defended by a ten-mile line of trenches and a strong force under Gen. Joseph Johnston. President Lincoln and War Secretary Edwin Stanton were pressuring McClellan to push ahead to Richmond, the grand prize—but the general held back. Before he could capture the rebel capital he would have to take Yorktown, lying across his path. And he wasn't sure what awaited him there.

George McClellan was a cautious campaigner— too cautious, many thought. He was also stubborn, refusing to move until his troops were well trained and he knew more about the enemy's defenses. So the Army of the Potomac stayed in place while the drilling and training went on.

None of this much mattered to Emma Edmonds. She would leave war strategy to others—she was content. Her disguise was working, the imp voice was silent, and she was having her moment in history. She'd also been lucky. Living at the hospital instead of in a crowded company tent had simplified matters. It was not only more comfortable, but more private, and she found it easier to hide her identity. Emma loved nursing. The doctors relied on her— and though she kept to herself, the other nurses treated cool, quiet Frank Thompson with friendly respect.

So Emma dozed peacefully on her cot, unaware that all this was soon to change—that two separate events would turn her tidy world completely upside down.

The first involved a Union agent who had been working in Richmond as a spy for McClellan. His mission was to get information about the rebel defenses in Yorktown. Growing careless, he'd been caught and, after a quick trial, shot by a Confederate firing squad.

The second event involved a Union patrol setting out that very night. The scout party, from Company B, consisted of four troopers and an officer named Vesey. It was a routine assignment to probe the enemy's outer defenses. With luck, the party might capture a rebel picket and bring him in for questioning. The men smeared dirt on their hands and faces to cut down their visibility and removed all loose metal that might clank or jingle. Then they slipped silently into the Virginia night.

There was nothing unique about either event. On the great, sweeping canvas of war, they were fairly minor episodes. But for Emma Edmonds, they were crucial. Taken together, these two events played a major part in her future, starting her on a path filled with risk and danger.

3

March 20, 1862

The following morning at work, Emma heard some surprising news. A trooper from Company B came to visit a sick friend, and the men talked about a newcomer to the trooper's outfit, a certain Lt. Vesey. Emma's ears perked up. Asking questions, she learned that the officer's first name was James and that he was a tall man with sandy hair and a bushy mustache.

"Where's he from?" she asked.

The rifleman shrugged. "Don't rightly know, Thompson. He transferred to us from a Boston company."

Emma broke into a grin. She'd known James Vesey when they were both living in Boston some years ago. They'd been good friends before Emma had gone off to Michigan and they'd lost touch. But she often thought of the big sandy-haired man, and the memory brought color to her face.

The other girls in Boston had sometimes teased her about being sweet on James, but in her blunt, straightforward way, Emma had laughed it off. Stuff and nonsense. She had much too much to do, and certainly no time for romantic interests. Yet here they both were, in the same regiment. Emma felt her cheeks reddening. Romance—fiddlesticks. She simply wanted to see her old friend again. Where was the harm in that?

When her shift ended, Emma washed up quickly, straightened her uniform, tilted her cap, and set off for the Company B area.

Hurrying along, she was surprised at the depth of her feelings. Well, she and James had enjoyed fine times together in Boston, and she'd missed him afterward. Quite a lot. He was so hearty and good-humored. He had a lovely way with him, always cheering her up when she needed it. Imagine finding him again—what a coincidence! Of course, she'd have to play out her role and pretend to be Frank Thompson, but maybe he wouldn't see through her disguise. In those days, she'd worn her hair long, in a bun at the nape of her neck; now it was short. The army uniform would help, and her face had matured quite a bit. She'd keep her cap low and hope for the best.

Bother, it *was* confusing. She might just let him

in on the secret anyway. Somehow she knew he'd understand and could be trusted. But she'd deal with all that later. Now she just yearned to see him, to talk to James and hear the booming laugh that always made her feel so warm and happy.

Outside the company headquarters' tents, pennants waved in the warm breeze. Excited, planning what she would say, she hurried along the line until she reached Company B. Some distance behind the last row of tents in a cleared field, Emma noticed a familiar ritual. A cluster of soldiers, bareheaded, stood around a mound of earth while the chaplain read a psalm. His voice carried to her on the breeze:

> *Commit thy way unto the Lord.*
> *Trust also in Him and*
> *He shall bring it to pass. . . .*

Emma stopped near a gunner who was leaning on an artillery piece, watching the service.

"Right sad 'bout Lt. Vesey," he muttered.

Emma froze. "Who?"

"Vesey," the gunner answered. "He took a patrol out for the first time last night. They ran into a big rebel party and there was a fight. Our lads got back safe, 'cept for the lieutenant. Took a musket ball in his neck. Dead by the time they brought 'im in."

> *The Lord knoweth*
> *The days of the upright,*
> *And their inheritance*
> *Shall be forever. . . .*

Emma walked numbly toward the group of mourners. Someone picked up a rough wooden cross and pushed it into the dirt at one end of the mound. Somebody else picked up a gold-braided hat and hung it on an arm of the cross.

> *For such as be blessed of Him*
> *Shall inherit the earth. . . .*

There was a mist across Emma's eyes. Through it she stared at the crude lettering: VESEY, J—LT., U.S.A. It couldn't be. It wasn't *possible.* Just minutes before she'd been hurrying to see him, to meet this man who'd meant so much to her—more than she'd ever realized. Emma added numbers—James must have been about thirty. Only three decades, and all that was left was a dirt mound lying at her feet like a grim joke. Time was a cheat. Now she'd never smile with him, or hear his voice, or warm to his laughter.

> *Wait on the Lord and keep His way,*
> *And He shall exalt thee*
> *To inherit the land. . . .*

Emma turned away feeling sick, the chaplain's words trailing after her. Her mouth was sour with the taste of pain. Slowly it turned to anger. There would be thousands of Veseys before this was over— thousands dead before the country was whole again. When she enlisted, she'd pictured herself starting on a fine, glorious adventure. Her way had seemed so safe and secure. But all that was a myth. In war there was no safety. Dirt mounds covered dreams as well as corpses.

"Took a musket ball in his neck. Dead by the time they brought him in. . . ."

Something began to stir in Emma. The imp was coming back to life, whispering, taunting her. For a while, she'd felt very pleased with her masquerade, even a little smug. Now those feelings were passing, and old fires were starting to smolder.

Fighting back tears, Emma stumbled blindly toward the hospital. Her path took her near a small cabin where the chaplain, Major Butler, lived with his wife. Emma knew Mrs. Butler, who often came to the hospital to visit patients and bring them treats from her kitchen. Emma and the older woman had become friends. Now, as she passed the cabin, some instinct drew her toward the front door. Suddenly she needed to talk, to see a kind face and hear a friendly voice. Distraught and barely aware of what she was doing, Emma stopped and knocked. Mrs. Butler opened the door, took one look at the young soldier standing there and drew him inside.

"Sit down, Franklin. Make yourself comfortable," she said, staring at Emma curiously. "I'll get us some hot coffee."

Emma drank the coffee gratefully, leaned back in her chair, and closed her eyes.

"Right sad 'bout Lt. Vesey. . . . Right sad 'bout Lt. Vesey. . . ."

All at once the tears came. Between her sobs she told Mrs. Butler about James—their friendship, her running to meet him, the shock of seeing the sad little grave. Emma's feelings overwhelmed her. Once started, she just couldn't stop—in next to no time, out poured the rest of her secret. She talked about her need to be in the war, about posing as a man, and confessed her true name and identity. With a rush of relief, she blurted out everything that had been bottled up inside for so long.

Mrs. Butler listened wide-eyed. "I declare," she murmured, half to herself. "I declare . . ." She came over, bent down, and put her arm around the young woman's shoulder.

"Franklin—I mean Emma—I expect you were sent to me today. Things like this aren't accidents. It's too heavy a burden for you to carry alone—time you had a friend and an ally."

Emma blinked in surprise and relief. "You're not going to turn me in?"

The chaplain's wife laughed. "My dear, I come from pioneer people. In '41 my folks drove a team and wagon from Independence clear to the Willamette Valley. We farmed the land when it was scarce more than a wilderness. That kind of thing puts iron in a woman." Mrs. Butler's eyes twinkled. "I confess, at first I was taken aback by your story. Lord, yes. But I do think you're a wonder." The gray-haired woman smiled and gazed out the little window. "If I were your age, I'm not sure I wouldn't try the same fool thing myself."

Staring at Mrs. Butler, Emma realized it wasn't finished after all; her secret was still safe. Hardly believing her good fortune, she wiped her nose, grinned at her new friend, and began talking again, filling in the details of her story.

By the time she left the cabin, Emma felt much

calmer. For a long time she'd been isolated and cut off; now she could share her secret with Mrs. Butler, a partner as strong as she herself. But grief still burned inside, and the imp voice was getting bolder, stirring her discontent. Until this morning she'd been satisfied being Frank Thompson, Union field nurse. Now it all seemed so trivial. She had a fierce need to do more, to strike a real blow for the cause. She wanted to avenge James's death—she *had* to. But how?

Emma fretted, but the glimmer of an answer came a few days later. A rumor sped through camp that one of the Union's key spies had been captured in Richmond and shot. McClellan had counted on this agent. Now the army was without eyes and ears, and someone had to fill the gap. Pressure from Washington was building, but the general refused to gamble. He insisted on more information before pushing ahead.

Busy with her chores, Emma took in all the talk and gossip. The more she heard, the more her interest grew. An idea was slowly forming—a wild notion pushing its way into her awareness. When she saw what was happening, she was alarmed. The whole idea was mad. A fantasy. Downright impossible! Yet here was the nagging voice again. Coaxing. Whispering. Daring her to take new risks.

Trust also in Him and
He shall bring it to pass. . . .

Emma's faith was strong. Weakness wasn't in
her nature. She'd faced fear many times—and was
ready to face it again. Of course the whole thing
might take more grit than she could muster. But
how could you know the limits of your courage if
you never put it to the test?

That night Emma hardly slept, tossing and turning, plagued by dreams of graves and crude crosses.
At dawn she awoke with a start, and her mind was
crystal clear. She had her answer: she would try the
impossible.

March 23, 1862

When Emma told her friend she wanted to become a spy, Mrs. Butler almost dropped the pan of biscuits she was holding.

Quickly she sat Emma down and tried hard to discourage her. It was one thing, she pointed out, to take risks as a battlefield nurse, but plain foolhardy to go *begging* for danger. The chaplain's wife did her very best, cajoling and arguing. But she sensed that it was of no use; she knew Emma was strong-willed, daring, dedicated—and stubborn as an old razorback hog.

Emma listened politely, her jaw set, her lips in a tight smile. She couldn't understand her friend's reaction. "I 'preciate your sentiments," she said at last, "but my mind's made up, Mrs. Butler. I'll do it—if they'll have me."

Faced with an irresistible force named Emma Edmonds, the chaplain's wife surrendered. "I expect you've taken leave of your senses," she sighed. "But I understand; people do what they must. If you're real set on this, at least the major and I can help."

Maj. Butler wasn't in on Emma's big secret. As far as he knew, she was simply young Frank Thompson, idealistic and hotheaded, and the chaplain agreed to serve as sponsor. He borrowed some army manuals from headquarters, and Emma spent her free hours learning about weapons, fortifications, makes of cannons, and types of projectiles. Then the major sent Pvt. Thompson's name in to McClellan's chief of staff.

The next day young Thompson faced a panel of stern-faced officers. They fired a barrage of questions at him until he felt like a fort under attack. They examined his background, experience, and knowledge of armaments. They probed his beliefs, patriotism, and feelings about the Union cause. They even put him through a "phrenological test." A solemn young captain, his cuffs turned up, felt the curves and bumps on Pvt. Thompson's head. Finally he gave the candidate high ratings for "bravery, secretiveness, and good character."

After a brief conference, the committee agreed to give the young soldier a chance. Thompson stood and took the special oath for secret agents, then met the adjutant who would be his contact and supply him with funds.

The officer came straight to the point. "You'll have a free hand, Thompson. Work behind the rebel lines any way you can. Get the facts we need and bring 'em back—plus yourself—in one piece. Be ready to start in three days."

Nervous and excited, Emma talked over her next step with Mrs. Butler. To move freely in enemy territory, she'd need a good disguise. The simplest, of course, would be to wear a Confederate uniform; she could easily piece one together from the prisoners. But that was risky. The Southern troopers would be curious. They might ask about her home town, or what outfit she belonged to, or the names of her officers. One false answer and she'd be finished.

Thinking about it, Emma soon found a better option. Everyone knew that the Confederate armies used a great many slaves to do heavy labor. Black work gangs dug trenches, built roads, cleaned stables, hauled wood and water. There were slaves everywhere—useful, but totally ignored. To rebel eyes, all slaves were faceless beings, invisible men who were hardly ever noticed. It was the perfect disguise. Black skin would be Emma's armor.

Once decided, she hitched a wagon ride to Fort

Monroe to buy what she needed at the post store. She put together her outfit quickly—except for one important item. To look convincing, she'd have to have a black woolly wig.

Parked on a bench outside the store, Emma wracked her brain, trying to remember where she had seen such a wig before. Then it came to her. While she was in Washington, she'd gone to a minstrel show. These shows, very popular in the capital, were performed by white men with their faces blackened. The "darkies" amused the crowd with songs, dances, banjo strumming, and lively humor. On stage they were dressed in fancy suits with big bow ties—and they all wore black woolly wigs.

Pvt. Thompson jumped up and ran toward the docks where ships, cruising Chesapeake Bay, linked Fort Monroe with the Union capital. The dockside was chaotic with new troops arriving, supplies being unloaded, and men driving army mules ashore from transport barges. He was in luck: the official mail boat for Washington was about to leave. Pushing through the crowd, he found the captain, pressed money into his hand, and asked him to buy a minstrel wig in the city.

The grizzled old sailor looked surprised. He'd been bribed at times to bring back whiskey, food, or special brands of tobacco—but a minstrel wig?

What in tarnation was *that* all about? Sensing his suspicion, Franklin snapped, "Secret orders from Gen. McClellan, and not a word to anyone!" At the commander's name, the boatman nodded nervously and touched his cap. Yes, yes, of course. He'd find a darky wig, a real good one, and bring it along the following afternoon.

By the third day—the adjutant's deadline—Emma had her wig. She gave Dr. Hodes a memo from headquarters detaching her from the hospital for "special assignment." Then, carrying her gear, she hurried to the cabin where her fellow conspirator was waiting. "Franklin Thompson" had served Emma well; a new personality was about to be born.

5

March 29, 1862

Emma stared into Mrs. Butler's mirror and broke out laughing. Looking out at her was a total stranger—a small, gawky, brown-skinned man with a crown of woolly black hair. He had on a gray flannel shirt, patched overalls, and a pair of ancient shoes several sizes too big. Around his neck he wore an old red bandanna.

Hands on her hips, Mrs. Butler regarded her friend critically. "I declare, Em, you look more like a darky than any I've seen in these parts."

Emma studied her image anxiously. "I pray the rebels think so, Mrs. Butler." She leaned forward and examined her skin. "I tried different kinds of colorings like iodine and tobacco juice, but the best was silver nitrate. I found some in the hospital, and made a solution of it in water." She held up a worn canvas sack. "I'm taking some with me in a little bottle, case I start to fade."

The chaplain's wife came over and put an arm around Emma's waist. In the mirror, wise old eyes gazed into lively young ones. "I knew I'd never get you to change your mind," she said quietly. "Knew it all along. You're a stubborn one and you'll do what you have to do. But stubborn's different from foolhardy. Be careful, girl."

Emma nodded. "I will, I promise."

Mrs. Butler slipped a packet into Emma's canvas sack. "Some corncakes and slices of dried apple," she said. "Lord knows what you'll find to eat over *there.*"

Emma smiled. Mrs. Butler made it sound as if she were going to California instead of a few miles up the peninsula. She swallowed hard and suddenly didn't trust herself to speak. Turning, she flung her arms around her gray-haired friend and supporter, holding her tight in a brief, desperate embrace. Then, with a wave, she darted out.

Leaving the cabin, Emma hurried along the row of officers' billets toward the headquarters' tent at the far end. She started past the field hospital and, on a sudden impulse, popped her head in through the open tent flap. Dr. Hodes was sitting there, working at the cluttered table. He seemed weary.

Emma deepened her voice.

" 'Scuse me, suh," she said.

The doctor looked up in annoyance. He stared at her for a long moment, while she held her breath. "Yes? What do *you* want?"

"Mah name Cuff, suh," Emma replied. "Lookin' fo' Mistuh Prahvit Thompson. Ah b'lieve he wuk here?"

"*Supposed* to work here," grumped Dr. Hodes, frowning at his intruder. "Don't know where the fool is. Gone off on some kind of special mission, I believe."

Emma bobbed her head and grinned. "Yassuh. He say, suh, he gon' gimme a ol' shirt."

The doctor turned back to his paperwork. "Well, I can't help you, Cuff. You'd better go along—and if you see Frank Thompson, tell him to get back here where he's needed."

"Yassuh, doctuh. Ah see 'im, ah tell 'im."

Emma ducked out of the tent and hurried on, suppressing a big grin. For weeks now she'd been with Doc Hodes, working at his side every single day. If *he* couldn't see through her disguise, maybe it would work after all.

Headquarters was the usual scene of bustle and activity, with aides and messengers hurrying to and fro. The adjutant, pacing to one side, was waiting for her. Emma stepped up and saluted, and he gaped in surprise.

"Thompson? By God, that's quite a rig you've dreamed up." He shook his head admiringly. "I'll wager you'd fool old Jeff Davis himself."

The officer pulled out a fat brass watch and popped open the cover. "Time to get started. My orders are to take you through our pickets. After that, you'll be on your own."

Together they cut east through the sprawling encampment, and Pvt. Thompson had to step lively to keep up with the adjutant's brisk strides. Darkness was beginning to settle over the tents and cook fires were being lit. Overhead, the first faint stars of evening winked on.

In silence, they made their way through the Company K bivouac area, past a battery of menacing siege guns. They circled behind the cavalry stables where she could hear the stamping of horses. Somewhere a trooper began playing a sad song on a harmonica. Emma knew the words well.

> *Farewell Mother, you may never*
> *Press me to your heart again.*
> *But oh, you'll not forget me mother,*
> *If I am numbered with the slain. . . .*

Ten more minutes of walking brought them to the outer edge of the Union position, with the York

River on its right flank. A sentinel, hardly more than a boy, raised his rifle and barred their way.

"Stand easy," the adjutant said. "We're passing this man through the lines, orders of Gen. McClellan."

The sentinel recognized the officer, saluted, and continued on his rounds. Emma and her escort found a low ridge and scrambled to the top. The adjutant turned and patted her shoulder. "From here you're on your own, Thompson," he said in a whisper. "I wish you good luck." Then he melted into the night.

Emma drew a long breath, suddenly feeling lonely and vulnerable. She bent down and shoved some slips of paper and a stub of pencil into her shoe. She'd need them to jot down the information the general wanted. Her hands and face were beginning to itch—probably due to the nitrate solution—but there was nothing she could do about it now. Crouching on the ridge, she stared across the valley toward the enemy lines. The lush fields had all been burned to stubble, to give the Yorktown defenders a clear line of fire. But some huckleberry bushes and several stands of loblolly pine still survived. She could use them for cover.

Beyond the trees, Emma made out distant campfires—the outer pickets of the Army of Northern

Virginia. Getting through this screen of rebel guards was her next challenge. She studied the pattern of the fires. They glowed and beckoned, sending a welcome and a warning.

The melancholy song crept into her thoughts again.

> *Just before the battle, Mother,*
> *I am thinking most of you.*
> *While upon the field we're waiting*
> *With the enemy in view. . . .*

The enemy was certainly in view—waiting just across the valley—and for the first time since she'd enlisted, Emma felt a creeping fear. Up till now, she'd hardly had time to fret or even think. She'd been too busy fantasizing and playacting. Now it was different—now her survival was at stake. Mrs. Butler's words came back to her. Lord, what *was* she doing here in this crazy disguise? Why had she given up her safe, comfortable spot at the hospital with Dr. Hodes to flirt with danger?

Bother—she knew perfectly well what she was doing and why. Hadn't she ached to avenge James's death? To support Lincoln and the cause, body and soul? To be a participant in history, not just a bystander? The imp voice was always there, prodding and urging her on. She could no more ignore it than she could stop herself from breathing.

Mother, hear the cry of freedom,
How it swells upon the air!
Yes, we'll rally 'round the standard,
Or we'll perish bravely there. . . .

Off to the left came a crackle of sniper fire. The sudden noise startled her, snapping her back to reality. Enough morbid thoughts—she'd act now and worry about it later.

A half-moon crept over the horizon, giving just enough dim light to help her. Narrowing his eyes, "Cuff" planned his route across the dangerous open zone. Then he whispered a quick prayer, scrambled down the ridge, and started across the valley.

6

March 30, 1862

It took Cuff several hours to get across the open zone. He would wait for scattered clouds to drift over the moon, then dart from bushes to trees, trees to bushes. Twice he heard the sharp crack of a musket but didn't know if he was the target, so he kept going. Drawing closer to the enemy lines, he watched and waited. The pickets plodded back and forth between the campfires, following a pattern. He timed himself carefully, then crouched and raced through a gap. A rebel sentry was only sixty feet away, but never noticed the lone black slave.

Inside the rim of defenses, Cuff could relax a bit. He trudged for a while through the woods until he reached a weedy footpath. The moon was gone now, and he decided to wait until morning before moving on.

Wearily Cuff crawled under a bush, stretched out, and soon fell asleep.

The yams will grow, the cotton blow,
We'll have the rice 'n' corn.
Oh, never you fear, some day you'll hear
Ol' Gabriel sound his horn. . . .

The sound of voices awakened Cuff. He peered through the bushes and saw some black men coming down the path. They were singing softly, carrying pans and buckets. Cuff was worried. Would the men accept him? He swallowed nervously—it was time to find out. He got up, brushed himself off, and stepped into view, wearing a sheepish grin. The slaves stopped in surprise at the sight of this small dark stranger who had popped out of nowhere.

Cuff nodded and scuffed his shoes. "Mawnin'," he said. "Mah name Cuff. Ah'm lost."

The men, dressed in old clothes like his own, grouped around, curious but friendly. They were taking breakfast to the sentries out on the picket lines. One of the men handed Cuff a piece of army biscuit and a tin cup of hot coffee.

"We be headin' back to camp in a little while," he said. "You want to come 'long, jus' wait here."

Thanking him, Cuff wolfed the biscuit and coffee and sat down again. Half an hour later, the slaves returned. He handed over the empty cup and fell into step with the party. There were eight of them;

nobody would notice one more black face. The men shambled along silently, Cuff walking with them. They reached the outskirts of Yorktown and the rebel encampment, where they headed toward a kitchen tent and went inside. Cuff held back, unsure of himself. He stood shuffling his feet, wondering what to do next. But before he could decide, a Confederate officer on a roan horse came trotting up. He stared at Cuff suspiciously.

"Why aren't you working?" he asked. "Who do you belong to?"

Cuff bobbed his head and put on his foolish smile. "Don' b'long to nobody, mastuh. Ah's free, far as ah know. Wantin' to go to Richmond, find some wuk."

The officer frowned. "There are no free niggers here," he growled. "Not while there's a Confederate army in Virginia." He turned and shouted to a trooper: "Sergeant! Put this cheeky rascal to work, and keep him at it. If he turns lazy, give him a good lesson with the lash!"

Spurring his horse, the officer wheeled and trotted off. The sergeant beckoned and Cuff followed dutifully. Passing through camp, he shuffled along with eyes half closed. But under the drooping, lazy lids, the eyes took sharp note of everything. The vast area reminded him very much of his own encampment, except that here the soldiers were dressed in gray instead of blue.

South of the city, the rebels were building defenses to hold off the Federal army. There was a long parapet over eight feet high, and scores of slaves were at work on it. Some were digging trenches and gun pits. Others pounded double rows of stakes into the ground. A third group filled this space with mountains of rocks and gravel. The sergeant pushed a shovel at Cuff and pointed to a large wheelbarrow. Cuff's duty was to fill the barrow with gravel, push it up an inclined plank to the top of the parapet, and dump the ballast between the stakes.

Even for a brawny man it would have been hard work. For small, slim Cuff, it soon became torture. Under a hot sun, shoulders aching, Cuff filled barrow after barrow. Then he forced each load up the tilted plank. The plank was narrow and wobbly, and sometimes the heavy barrow tipped off. When that happened he had to climb down, refill it, and start over again. The men around him worked steadily. Now and then they traded a little banter or broke into a soulful hymn. But most of the time they worked in sad silence.

Noontime brought a chance to rest and eat. Cuff picked up a tin bowl and spoon and joined the long line, glad to be free of the wheelbarrow. He soon discovered that the white troopers ate well, but slave food was poor—mostly cornbread and gruel, with a bit of dried beef now and then. Later the work gangs went back to their drudgery. The sergeants who supervised them were harsh men: they bullied and threatened, and any slave who slowed down felt the sharp pain of a leather lash. Cuff worked as hard as he could, hoping to avoid attention, and by mid-afternoon his hands were raw and bleeding. But the sun went down at last and work on the fortifications ended for the day.

After a skimpy supper, the slaves were allowed one hour to wander around freely. Then they had to report to an area at the far end of camp. Cuff took good advantage of his free time, roaming the fort, noting the types of artillery, memorizing the layout of the trenches. He tried to remember everything so he could jot it down later.

At curfew hour, all the blacks were herded into a compound for the night, and Cuff saw with relief that there were no white overseers here. The slaves broke up into small groups. They sprawled under scraps of canvas hung from branches, and started fires to boil water for acorn coffee. Cuff with his brown skin had been accepted completely, and during the day had become friendly with some of the others. But now he needed privacy. A kindly old man handed him a ragged blanket, which he took gratefully. Then he found an isolated tree, sat down, and tried to ignore his aches and pains.

When all was quiet and nobody was watching, Cuff drew out his slips of paper and began to write in the dark. He listed the artillery he had seen on his walk: twenty-five rifled three-inch cannons . . . eleven Dahlgren guns . . . twenty-nine thirty-two pounders . . . seven siege howitzers . . . fourteen heavy mortars . . . thirteen Columbiads . . . many light weapons. He made a rough diagram of the new earthworks, then pushed all the slips back under the lining of his shoe.

Cuff was pleased. His fears had faded. His information was just what McClellan needed. He'd spend one more day here with the enemy, then figure a way—somehow—to get back to the Union lines. Lying on his blanket, Cuff suddenly thought of his color. In the gloom, he slipped the bottle of brown solution from his sack and dabbed his face and hands. Then, munching some of Mrs. Butler's apple slices, he settled down for the night.

Twenty yards away, a group of slaves sat hunched over a campfire. As Cuff dozed they started singing in low soft voices. It was the very hymn he'd heard early that morning in the woods. Quietly he sat up and crept closer to the firelight.

Praise and thanks! The Lord he come
To set His people free . . .
Some may call it Day of Doom,
For us 'tis Jubilee . . .
The Lord who bade the Red Sea part
Is now as strong as then . . .
He say one word, and all the slaves
Will be the Lord's free men. . . .

Others joined in the chorus, their voices blending in subtle harmony.

The yams will grow, the cotton blow,
We'll have the rice 'n' corn.
Oh, never you fear, some day you'll hear ·
Ol' Gabriel sound his horn.

After a while Cuff slipped back to his blanket under the tree. He would need his rest for the day ahead. Lulled by the melodic voices, he fell asleep at last—his head filled with thoughts of work and sweat, of hope and faith and the courage of black men.

7

March 31, 1862

Early in the morning, the slaves were roused, given a quick breakfast, and sent to their work areas. Cuff felt better, but his hands were still torn and blistered. He knew he couldn't last an hour digging gravel on the parapet and wrestling with the barrow. But if he complained to one of the guards, he'd be asking for trouble. Looking around, he saw a husky young man who was one of the kitchen squad. Cuff fell into step with him, showed him his hands, and explained the problem. The young man was sympathetic and agreed to exchange places with Cuff for the day. To seal their bargain Cuff gave him a small rusty penknife that he'd brought in his sack. Smiling with pleasure, the man headed toward the trenches while Cuff joined the slaves waiting at the cook tent.

The spy's second day behind the lines was much

less painful than the first. He was assigned to a group that took meals to the crews manning the heavy artillery. Since these posts were spread out along the Confederate front, it gave him a chance to learn more about the fortifications. He eavesdropped on the conversations around him and learned that fresh reinforcements were expected. He also heard that Gen. Robert E. Lee had visited Yorktown and didn't think the defenses would hold against a strong Union attack. All of this, he knew, would be of interest at McClellan's headquarters.

During the afternoon, while carrying pots and buckets with a slave named Jabez, Cuff saw a long row of fat logs lined up behind banks of earth. They were pointed south, and soldiers were busy painting them black.

"What's them logs fo'?" he asked his companion.

"They's Quaker guns," Jabez replied.

Cuff didn't have to playact—his puzzlement was real.

"Ah never heard o' no Quaker guns befo'."

Jabez grinned. "Quakers is ver' religious people, Cuff. Peace-lovin'. They don't hold with no wars. They won't do no shootin', see? An' neither will them guns."

Studying the painted logs, Cuff realized how

convincing they would look when seen through a Union telescope. He made a mental note to pinpoint the fake cannons on his secret map.

Several hours later, he and Jabez were filling canteens at a pump for one of the gun crews. Nearby, he noticed a heavyset gentleman in dark civilian clothes talking to a group of officers. Cuff recognized him as a peddler—supposedly a good friend and strong Union sympathizer. He often came to the Union camp with his wagon, staying for hours on some pretext or other. Straining his ears, Cuff caught some of the man's conversation. He was so surprised he had to fight to keep himself from spinning around and staring. The man was a clever Confederate spy who picked up data on his peddler trips, then passed it to the rebels! Bending over the pump, Cuff heard him boasting of his success in luring Union patrols into ambushes, causing the death of many.

The young woman thought of James Vesey and felt herself go hot with pain and anger. The rebel agent was talking away, unaware that he was doomed—but Emma wasted no sympathy on him. Her cause was just, she had a job to do, and fate had thrust this turncoat into her hands. She'd report the peddler to headquarters; his next visit to the Union lines would be his last visit anywhere.

Slowly the long day passed. Then the sun dipped

to the horizon and Cuff began making plans. He had a lot of valuable information and had to get back as quickly as possible, but it wouldn't be easy. Slipping into the rebel camp was simpler than finding a way to break out of it. Except for his hour of liberty, he had no time alone, and at night he'd be penned with the other blacks in their compound. If he was caught outside that area, he'd be shot as a spy or hanged as a slave attempting to escape. And neither option was very appealing.

During his free hour, Cuff wandered toward the picket line west of the new parapet. Here the gap between the two forces was less than a mile. He knew that in emergencies reliable black men were allowed briefly to stand picket duty. Perhaps a black guard could be convinced—or bribed—to let him slip through.

Cuff drew closer to the outposts. Suddenly a young Confederate lieutenant came striding toward him, a frown on his face, his red mustache bristling. Cuff swallowed hard and got ready for trouble. "You, boy!" the lieutenant barked. "Come along with me."

The officer marched Cuff to a forward position, and the trooper in charge saluted smartly. "Corporal," the lieutenant said, "put this one in the post where the man was shot. He'll do for now, until I can send up a proper replacement."

When he left, the corporal looked at Cuff angrily. "I don't hold with lettin' your kind up here, but orders is orders." He shoved a handsome rifle into Cuff's hands; Cuff recognized it as an Enfield Carbine. "Know what this is? It's a rifle. All primed and loaded," the corporal growled. "All you gotta do is aim 'n' pull the trigger."

Cuff bobbed his head and smiled. "Yessuh, ah unnerstan'. Ah knows how to use 'er."

The corporal shoved Cuff roughly toward a small mound. "Stand there, keep your eyes open, fire at anything in the valley that moves." He narrowed his cold eyes. "You fall asleep on duty, boy, we'll shoot you like a dawg."

Cuff shook his head. "Don' worry none, suh. Ah won't fall asleep—too *scared* tuh fall asleep."

The corporal was gone before Cuff finished his sentence. Elated, he looked around, marveling at his wonderful luck. The sentries on each side were fifty or sixty feet away. No problem there, but he'd have to move soon before the lieutenant came back with a substitute. In minutes a misty drizzle began. Clouds bunched overhead. Night closed in and Cuff could no longer see the other pickets. Clutching his rifle, he stepped from the mound and tiptoed into the valley.

The gloom and mist were so heavy now that he

could barely see two feet ahead. Catlike and silent, he slipped through the night, knowing that any sudden noise would bring a dozen shots crashing in his direction. Following his instincts, Cuff snaked across the open zone until he sensed that the Union lines were just ahead. But a night arrival was risky and he didn't relish drawing sentry fire.

Soaked to the skin, the weary spy crawled under a sheltering bush to wait for morning.

8

April 1, 1862

The day dawned dry and clear. A bored sentry, tired after a long, wet night of guard duty, looked across the valley and blinked in surprise. Coming toward him was a small man in torn overalls. He had a mop of woolly hair, his skin was streaked brown, and he was waving a red bandanna tied to a mud-stained rifle.

Cuff cut off the young soldier's bumbling questions. "Get your lieutenant," he said crisply. "I have urgent business at headquarters."

Some ten minutes later, agent Franklin Thompson was sitting across from his contact, Col. Shrub. The adjutant waited in suspense, tapping his fingers anxiously on the desk. With a grin, Thompson pulled off his shoe and spread out his notes and diagrams. For the next half hour, he briefed the colonel on everything he'd seen and done. He described the different gun batteries, the new fortifications, the size of the enemy encampment. He told the colonel about the fake cannons, and finally of the rebel spy who'd been posing for months as a friendly peddler.

The adjutant, delighted with the report, asked Thompson to wait while he went to inform Gen. McClellan. Some time later, the commander himself came to shake Thompson's grimy hand and personally thank him for all he'd accomplished. Pvt. Thompson was dazed and flattered; then he remembered the handsome Enfield Carbine. He started to put it on the desk, but the adjutant waved it away. "Keep the rifle, Thompson," he said. "You've earned a souvenir."

Later in the chaplain's cabin, Emma Edmonds scrubbed off the remaining brown stain and changed into her regular uniform. It was a luxury for her to be clean again and in familiar clothes. Mrs. Butler, overjoyed, bustled about the kitchen, and over a mug of coffee and a bracing bowl of hot soup, Emma finally relaxed. While her friend listened in amazement, Emma recounted her adventures, careful to avoid the military secrets. The chaplain's wife beamed happily. "The major and I prayed for you night and day," she said, going to the door with Emma. "I walked beside you, my dear. Praise the Lord it's all over and you've got it out of your system." Emma smiled and hugged her friend, but said nothing.

Pvt. Thompson's welcome at the medical tent was less joyous, but he knew Dr. Hodes was pleased to have him back. " 'Bout time you turned up," the doctor grumbled. "Don't know or care what all that tomfoolery was, but I'll remind you that I'm trying to run a hospital. We have a great deal of work to do here, and I venture we'll have even more before too long."

The doctor's words were prophetic. Thompson's report, plus information from captured rebels, gave McClellan the facts he needed; three days after the private's return, McClellan ordered an all-out attack. The Confederate generals knew they were outnumbered and outgunned; Quaker cannons might fool enemy eyes, but they couldn't stop an advance. The rebels began to fall back. But farther to the north, Gen. Joseph Johnston had built up a large army for a drive on Washington. He quickly detached thousands of these men and rushed them south to defend Yorktown.

Within sight of their goal, the Union troops were stopped and had to dig in for a long siege. Every day brought fierce new battles and skirmishes—and many new casualties. The hospital, once calm and placid, became a scene of hectic, feverish activity. As wounded men came flooding in, all regular nursing shifts were dropped. Franklin and the others worked around the clock, taking time only for a quick meal and a few hours of exhausted sleep. To the steady rumble of gunfire, he assisted the surgeons at the operating table, cleaned and dressed wounds, carried food and water to suffering patients, and tried to comfort the dying.

Emma's war, no longer a grand colorful pageant, became a nightmare of endless fighting, bleeding bodies, and weary men. But through it all, she clung to her belief in the Union's cause and its future.

The siege dragged on until the Army of the Potomac finally took Yorktown at the beginning of May—five weeks after Pvt. Thompson's spy mission. Fighting a stubborn rearguard action, the rebels headed north and the Union troops followed. In different parts of the country, other major battles were taking place, but on the Virginia peninsula, McClellan's men fought their way slowly toward the Confederate capital.

Then a period of heavy rain began. Torrents turned the roads to mud, slowing the advance. The mud got so deep that the artillery and supply trains took thirty-six hours to move a short five miles. Soon the Union forces faced yet another obstacle: the Chickahominy River, stretching from Williamsburg to a point east of Richmond. By mid-May, parts of the river were in Union hands, but much was still under rebel control.

Gen. McClellan ordered a bridge built across this barrier, out of range of enemy cannon fire. The bridge had to be large enough to carry horse-drawn artillery as well as foot soldiers. It would take weeks to finish. Meanwhile the Southerners were improving their defenses.

At Union headquarters, the officers studied their maps and shook their heads. It was downright irritating. In some places, Federal troops were only three miles from Richmond; at other points, the front was vague and uncertain. Of course the rebels would fight like fiends to protect their capital. But where would they make their stand? What types of defenses were they setting up? Everyone agreed that more information was needed. A daring agent would have to slip across the Chickahominy, penetrate the enemy lines, and bring back the answers. But who could do the job? Discussing the possibilities, McClellan remembered the success of young Frank Thompson at the battle of Yorktown. Quickly he sent for the adjutant, Col. Shrub.

Meanwhile, Pvt. Thompson kept up his weary rounds at the hospital, nursing the sick and wounded—completely unaware that he was on the brink of another strange and dangerous mission.

May 20, 1862

The moon was curtained with thick clouds. Wind rustled the willow trees along the Chickahominy. Now and then came the faint grumble of far-off cannon fire.

A rowboat slipped silently through the dark, pieces of blanket tied around the oars to keep them from splashing. When the boat reached the opposite river bank, a heavy middle-aged woman climbed out. She waved to the oarsman. He raised a hand in salute, turned his boat, and headed back to the far shore.

The woman, carrying a wicker basket, looked around to get her bearings. She knew from maps that the great Chickahominy swamp was on her left. If she followed its edge through the woods, she'd reach a dirt road winding away from the river. With a nod, the woman started off. Her long skirt made walking through the underbrush difficult, and branches snagged the basket she carried. After a mile or so, she found the road—a dim, gray band in the darkness. Here she would stay until dawn; then she'd head for the Confederate lines.

The tired woman sat down and leaned gratefully against a tree. Emma Edmonds, alias Franklin Thompson, alias Cuff the contraband slave, was now an Irish peddler named Bridget O'Shea. Her new disguise—and cover story—had been carefully worked out in the chaplain's cabin.

"I can't go back as Cuff," Emma had explained to Mrs. Butler. "Remember, that rebel officer left me standing guard duty. If Cuff showed up, he might be recognized. They could arrest him for deserting his post."

Mrs. Butler nodded, and the two friends lapsed into silence. Suddenly the older woman jumped up, hurried into the bedroom, and came back dragging an old campaign trunk.

"I brought a deal of fancy clothes with me from Baltimore," she said. "Lord knows I can't use them in this rough place, but *you* can."

Together they rummaged through the trunk, and soon Emma was transformed from an ordinary soldier into a plump, bosomy matron. Mrs. Butler tied a pillow around Emma's middle for bulk. Then came a petticoat, a fancy blouse, and a heavy skirt that reached the floor. Over all of this went a sweater and a fringed shawl. Mrs. Butler dusted flour in Emma's dark hair to turn it gray, then tied a big bonnet on her head. She stood back and studied the results. "One more touch," she announced. Poking in her sewing box, she found her extra pair of metal-rimmed eyeglasses and perched them on Emma's nose. "Perfect," she said. "Let them slide a bit, and look over the top."

To complete the disguise, Emma filled a basket with peddler's goods for the Southern soldiers—spools of thread, needles, matches, a pair of scissors, pieces of soap, corncakes, and packets of tea. Looking at herself in Mrs. Butler's mirror, Emma grinned. She liked the overall effect. Thousands of Irish immigrants had recently come to America, fleeing the terrible potato famine. Many had settled in this part of the country, so it was a safe cover. If anyone asked questions, she'd say she was from Providence Forge and had left a few jumps ahead of the advancing Yankees.

Now, having reached the winding road, Bridget O'Shea settled down to wait for morning. The humming of the wind made her drowsy, and she quickly dozed off. At first light she awoke, feeling stiff. The wind had risen sharply and the sky was thick with clouds; a storm was coming. Rising to her feet,

Bridget twitched her skirt in place and started on her way. Fat drops of rain began to fall, making small circles in the dust. Soon the rain was coming down heavily.

The peddler trudged through the mud, trying to stay under the trees along the road. But the wind whipped the rain sideways, drenching her. Coming around a bend, she saw an old frame house up ahead. There were no lights and it appeared to be abandoned. She quietly climbed the steps, carefully opened the door, and slipped inside. The house was deserted. The floor sagged. There was no furniture and the walls were streaked with ancient dirt. Grateful to have a roof over her head, Bridget pulled off her bonnet and soggy shawl. Lord, what a downpour—what a bother.

Suddenly she froze. Someone was groaning in the next room!

Creeping to the doorway, she peeked inside. A soldier lay on the bare floor—a Confederate officer. He appeared to be no more than a boy, and she could tell he was very sick. Kneeling at his side, she touched his forehead. He was burning up, his breath coming in gasps. His pulse was weak and there were red blotches on his face. Bridget knew the symptoms—she'd seen them often enough in camp. Typhoid fever was a killer that took no sides.

In both armies, the disease was doing more harm than all of the bullets, swords, and shellfire.

The young man stirred. "Water . . ."

In the kitchen, Bridget found some old crockery on a shelf. She filled a cup from the pump and hurried back to the soldier. The man drank thirstily and fell back gasping. He clutched at her hand. "Thank you, aunt."

The soldier's kit lay beside him. Bridget pulled out the blanket, folded it, and tucked it under the young man's head. Then she sat down near him. She was a firm believer in duty. Military orders were important, but this was important, too. Rebel or not, she couldn't walk away and let him die alone. She'd have to stay and keep a vigil—though she didn't think it would be for long.

All morning Bridget O'Shea sat with the dying boy. She tore a wide strip from her petticoat, moistened it, and placed the cool pad on his forehead. He reached for her hand again. She held his hand and sang to him—old hymns and lost lullabies she dimly remembered from childhood.

There wasn't much else she could do. She gave him more water, and in the afternoon she stirred a fire in the iron stove and made tea for them both. She also shared corncakes with her companion, though he could eat little. The tea revived him briefly. He raised himself on one elbow and stared at his guardian curiously. Had he somehow seen through her disguise? Well, it didn't matter; there was nothing he could do now.

The soldier was sinking. His voice came in gasps and whispers, and bit by bit she heard his story. Allen Hall was a lieutenant in a Virginia rifle company. He'd been ill for weeks with typhoid and had tried to carry on. Two days before, at Cold Harbor, his men had fought a battle with an advance Union force. The Virginians retreated, but Hall was too sick to keep up with them. Afraid of falling into enemy hands, he'd dragged himself off through the woods, where he'd found this house and managed to crawl inside.

For a time he slipped into a coma. Later, he roused himself. "Aunt," he whispered, "if you ever pass through the Confederate camp this side of Richmond, ask for a Maj. McKee of Gen. Ewell's staff. There's a gold watch in my pocket. Please give him the watch—he'll know who it should be sent to." The boy's eyes were glassy. "Tell the major—oh, just say I had a mind to go home. . . ."

Bridget O'Shea kept her vigil as the day faded into darkness. Outside, the storm raged. Rain drummed on the windows. Thunder growled. Somewhere in the house, a loose shutter went *slap*. . .

slap. . . slap. And, above it all, the wind moaned, keening for dying troopers.

Bridget stood up and stretched. Her back and shoulders ached. She walked to the window, stared at nothing, and went back to her soldier. She was feeling restless and weary. The sounds of the storm—rising and falling—slowly created their own music. A new hymn was making the rounds of the Union camps—a song written only a few months before by a Boston woman named Howe. Emma had found the stanzas printed in a magazine called *The Atlantic Monthly* and she'd heard it sung around the Union campfires. The glorious words were captivating, resounding in the drumming of horses' hooves, the rattle of caisson wheels, the blare of bugles and the crash of guns. Alone with her dying soldier, she heard them again in the sounds of the wind.

> *He is trampling out the vintage*
> *where the grapes of wrath are stored. . . .*

Lt. Hall muttered in delirium. She bathed his face with a cool cloth. Sitting against the wall, she held his thin hand and willed him some of her strength.

> *He has loosed the fateful lightning*
> *of His terrible swift sword. . . .*

She wondered when, if ever, this fearful war would end. A friend of the Butlers had just come from Washington. He told them President Lincoln had aged ten years over the last few months.

> *He has sounded forth the trumpet*
> *that shall never call retreat. . . .*

Now they were dying—the fine boys of both armies—gallants Lincoln had called "the brave and early fallen."

> *He is sifting out the hearts of men*
> *before His judgment seat. . . .*

Darkness finally came and Bridget O'Shea slept fitfully. She dozed on and off, haunted by painful dreams. In the gray light of morning, the young man was dead.

For a while she sat there, unable to move. With an effort she roused herself, found the gold watch, and put it in her basket. Then she covered the soldier with his blanket and said a silent prayer. She'd find Maj. McKee for him if it was the last thing she ever did.

Gathering her belongings, Bridget left the house,

closing the door gently behind her. According to her reckoning, the rebels would be several miles farther to the west. She headed slowly down the road, sidestepping the worst of the puddles. The rain had long since stopped, but her face was wet. She reached up and brushed the tears away.

Devil take this ugly war. It was brutal and cruel, yet she knew the Union had to survive. For her, that was all that mattered—it was the one thing she could believe in. She willed herself to stop thinking of young Lt. Hall. He was at peace now, but she still had work to do. At headquarters, Col. Shrub had shown her the secret battle map, stuck with its colored pins. "This area is a question mark," he said, poking a stubby finger at one spot. "Your mission, Thompson, is to find out what's going on here. We *must* know what tricks they're up to."

In her mind Bridget reviewed her orders—all the details and all the dangers—and fear began to creep in. Could she really carry it off? Would the disguise work this time? Would her luck hold, or was she tempting fate?

Oh be swift my soul to answer him,
be jubilant my feet.
His day is marching on. . . .

She brushed aside her morbid thoughts. Bother the risks. She wasn't a timid peddler woman—she was a Union soldier and proud of it.

Bridget O'Shea set her chin, wiped her nose, yanked her bonnet straight, and pushed on toward the enemy lines.

10

May 22, 1862

The Richmond road had numerous twists and branchings, and Bridget began to fear she'd lost her way. Suddenly a voice barked, "Halt!"

A sentry in Confederate gray stepped from the bushes and came toward her suspiciously. But as he drew near, his frown softened. What he saw was a harmless middle-aged woman, her clothes bedraggled, her face pale, her eyes red from crying. The woman explained that she had come to sell her goods in camp, but now she had another purpose. "I must find a staff officer named McKee," she said. "I have a message for him from a dying soldier."

Minutes later Miss O'Shea was bouncing along in a supply wagon pulled by an old mule. The driver helped her down outside Gen. Ewell's headquarters, where a sympathetic aide listened to her story. "I'm to give this gold watch to Maj. McKee," she explained. "It was the boy's last request."

The aide shook his head. The major was out with a surveying party and wouldn't be back until afternoon. "Meanwhile," he said, "make yourself comfortable, ma'am. You're welcome to the hospitality of our camp, such as it is." He led her to a tent where some black women were hard at work cooking and washing, and beckoned to one. "Take care of this lady, Rachel," he said. "See that she's comfortable and has something to eat."

Alone with the women, Bridget sat down on an empty crate and watched. They were a lively bunch, smiling and chattering, and now and then they would steal curious glances in her direction. One of them brought her two thick slices of bread made of rice and cornmeal, and a mug of sweet cider. She learned that they were contrabands—slaves who had wandered from their farms and plantations in the confusion of the war. Some contrabands made their way north; others, like this group, had been rounded up and put to work for the Confederate army. These women did the cooking and laundering for the staff at the rebel headquarters. Like many Southern house servants, they were treated far better than the field laborers and trench diggers Cuff had met before.

Wolfing her food, Bridget studied the slaves' clothing—bandannas tied neatly around their heads, aprons hitched around long, ragged skirts—making a mental note of it. It would be a useful disguise for a future mission. Listening to the gossip, she also learned about the units stationed there, the number of troops, and the names of their officers. This time she had decided to keep information in her head instead of writing it down. It would be much safer and would be good training for her.

At first the women were a bit shy as Bridget sat with them, but gradually they relaxed. Someone started to sing, and one by one the others joined in:

> *We are climbin' Jacob's ladder,*
> *We are climbin' Jacob's ladder,*
> *We are climbin' Jacob's ladder,*
> *Soldiers of the cross. . . .*

Bridget knew the hymn well. Softly, she joined them in the final chorus.

> *We are climbin' higher, higher,*
> *We are climbin' higher, higher,*
> *We are climbin' higher, higher,*
> *Soldiers of the cross.*

She sat a while longer, thinking of a deserted house and a dying man. Then, thanking the black women, she picked up her basket and stepped out to explore the area.

To her relief, she found she could move around with complete freedom. Nobody was suspicious of a poor woman trying to peddle her basket of meager goods. In fact, she sold quite a few packets of thread and pieces of soap to the friendly troopers. She also kept her eyes and ears open, talking to the soldiers, counting the various cannons, noting the layout of the defenses. All this was stored in her head; she'd have much to report when she got back to camp . . . *if* she got back to camp. There were no exact plans for her return, but she tried not to worry about that.

Three o'clock came, and with it, Maj. McKee. Bridget met him, turned over the gold watch, and described what had happened. The major was saddened. He shook his head and chewed the end of his droopy mustache. "Poor Allen Hall, rest his soul," he mused. "We wondered what became of the lad. At least he didn't fall into enemy hands."

The major excused himself with a bow, hurried into the headquarters tent, and returned a minute later.

"Ma'am," he asked, "can you ride?"

Bridget nodded. "Been riding since I was a shaver, sir. Had my own farm pony back in Country Clare."

McKee chewed his mustache again. "Then we'd much appreciate it if you'll grant a favor. We're right anxious to bring Lt. Hall's body in and give it a decent burial. If it's not imposin', you think you could guide a squad out to that old house?"

The spy's heart leapt at the prospects and possibilities opening up for her. She smiled sweetly. "I'd be right proud to take them, Major."

A fine-looking chestnut horse was led from the corral. A trooper made a step with his linked hands, and she climbed into the saddle. She usually sat her horses astride, the way men did, but just in time she remembered to sit sidesaddle, legs together in a ladylike manner. A sergeant rode up beside her and touched his cap. Behind him came the mule wagon, carrying four soldiers and a wooden coffin.

McKee gave the sergeant last-minute instructions. "We have reports of Union patrols this side of the river. Move with care, Parker, and look after this brave lady."

The party started off at last, with Bridget and the sergeant in front and the wagon following. At first she worried about finding the right way back, but soon began to recognize landmarks. As they rode along she did some more probing.

"You think the Yankees will attack soon?" she asked her companion.

Parker spat tobacco juice and grinned. "I believe so, ma'am. They'll head this way soon's they finish buildin' their bridge—but we'll be ready for 'em." He swept a hand toward the dense foliage on both sides of the river. "We're hidin' lots of heavy guns here in the woods. When the Yanks come down this road they'll march straight into an ambush. Purely won't know what hit 'em."

Miss O'Shea tried to look pleased. But she filed the alarming news in her head; it was something headquarters would certainly be glad to learn.

The rescue party took a wrong turn and had to backtrack, but they finally reached the old house. A soldier hopped from the wagon, looked inside, and reported that the body was still there under its blanket. As the men began unloading the coffin, Sgt. Parker turned to his guide. "I'd be much obliged, ma'am, if you could ride up to the next bend and kind of act as lookout. Watch for stray Yanks. If I sent one of my men, they'd shoot 'im for sure—but they'll never bother you."

Bridget's eyes lit up. "Don't you fret, Sergeant. I'll keep watch. When you're ready, just start back without me and I'll catch up."

Marveling once more at her good luck, the young spy trotted half a mile down the road and slid around the bend. Once out of sight, she swung her right leg over the pommel of the saddle, then kicked the horse into a fast canter. Horse and rider raced down the road as she put distance betwcen herself and the rebels.

After several miles she noticed that the swamp had narrowed greatly. She could even glimpse the Chickahominy through the trees. She wheeled the chestnut sharply, plunged through the underbrush, then straight into the river. The little horse was a sturdy swimmer, strong and confident. Nearing the Union side, she tore off her bonnet and waved it to attract the pickets' attention.

In a short while, Bridget O'Shea was back at headquarters, sitting across from Col. Shrub, telling him what she'd learned. The adjutant was delighted with her report. He also admired the chestnut horse she had ridden to safety. "He's all yours, Thompson," he said. "Add him to your collection of trophies."

Later, while changing clothes at the cabin, Emma brought Mrs. Butler up to date. Then she remembered something. "Oh, Lord!" she wailed. "I plumb forgot your lovely wicker basket. It's back at the rebel camp!"

The chaplain's wife laughed. "No matter. If you ask me, a basket for a horse is a good trade."

The women went out to look at the little chestnut tethered near the cabin, cropping grass. "He's a handsome animal, Em," said Mrs. Butler. "What are you going to name him?"

Emma grinned. "Rebel," she said.

11

May 30, 1862

The secret orders from Gen. McClellan were clear and concise:

Upon advancing beyond the Chickahominy, the troops will go prepared for battle at a moment's notice. All vehicles will be left on the eastern side of the river with the exception of ambulances.

The men will leave their knapsacks with the wagons and will carry three days' rations. Arms will be put in perfect order. All cartridge cases will carry forty rounds, with twenty additional rounds carried by the men in their pockets. Commanders of batteries will see that limber and caisson boxes are filled to their utmost capacity.

With the bridge completed and all preparations made, the Army of the Potomac launched its big attack on the nerve center of the Confederate government. Pvt. Thompson and his fellow soldiers were hoping for a quick, clean victory, but that wasn't to be. The Southern troops, fighting for a cause they believed noble and just, resisted fiercely. For days the battle raged back and forth, in and around the river. Finally a Union corps under Gen. Fitz-John Porter won several key victories and cut the railroad lines carrying supplies to Richmond.

Things looked promising for McClellan until nature took an unexpected hand. A great storm hit the peninsula. Sheets of rain fell night and day, flooding the valley and turning the calm river into a raging torrent. Mud on the Richmond road was over a foot deep. The storm badly damaged the new Union bridge and wrecked a second bridge that was being built.

By June, the rebels had been well reinforced and were able to counterattack. The Union troops lost ground before Richmond and the battlefield became fragmented, with pockets of men fighting everywhere.

During those weeks Pvt. Thompson's work took a new turn. Headquarters had been impressed with his success as a spy and also with his horsemanship. He was a fine rider, skilled and daring, and good messengers were badly needed. So to the complete annoyance of Dr. Hodes, Frank Thompson was again called from the hospital, this time to be a special courier for the Union generals who were directing the confused fighting.

Mounted on Rebel, Pvt. Thompson traveled the countryside for days, carrying orders and dispatches through swamp and mud, over rain-drenched fields and across streams swollen into rivers. Rebel was equal to every demand made on him, and Thompson enjoyed the excitement of his role. He also had his share of narrow escapes.

Once, coming back from a mission, the courier fell in with a Union cavalry patrol. There were four troopers, and Franklin was glad to have company. Suddenly shots flew at them from the nearby foliage. The patrol was being ambushed—not by the enemy, but by a band of renegade soldiers. Renegades, found on both sides, were armed guerrilla bands who operated without orders, completely on their own. Also called bushwhackers, they were supposed to be partisans of either the North or the South. But most of the time they were merely pirates, preying on civilians and soldiers; killing, robbing, and looting for their own gain.

Pvt. Thompson and his cavalry friends were outnumbered, but in the confusion were able to fight their way out of the trap. Several of the men were wounded and Rebel received a gash across his flank.

But he managed to limp back to camp with Franklin, where his minor wound was lovingly attended to.

Another time, heading home near rebel territory, Thompson decided to take a shortcut. Riding through an unfamiliar area, he somehow lost his way. Then, across a large open field, he spotted a column of Federal troops marching by. They were unmistakable in their blue uniforms. With a whoop, he turned the chestnut and cantered in their direction. Several men waved to him and he waved back in greeting. Suddenly a squad of enemy cavalrymen came charging out of the woods. Franklin realized in alarm that the soldiers in blue were prisoners. They hadn't been waving to him, but trying to warn him away! More enemy troopers appeared. Thompson wheeled his horse and headed back the way he had come, but another squad came charging at him. Turning again, he galloped toward the far end of the wide field—the only escape route still open.

Slowly his pursuers closed the gap. They began firing, and he heard shots whining past his ears. Then he felt a harsh sting in his right arm. Looking down, he saw that his sleeve was torn and blood was seeping out. His arm began to throb, but he gripped the reins tightly and kept going. Then Thompson froze. Directly ahead was a ditch wide and deep, and there was no way around it. He'd never jumped Rebel before; now he had no choice.

Leaning over the little horse's flying mane, he dug in his heels and whispered, "Up and over, Reb! Up and over!"

The ditch came closer and closer. The chestnut lifted high into the air. Thompson held his breath, leaning forward to keep himself balanced. There was a moment of peril as Rebel scrambled for his footing on the far side. Then on he galloped! Thompson patted Rebel proudly on his arched neck and looked back. His pursuers had pulled up short, unwilling to risk the jump for just one more prisoner.

Horse and rider found their way home at last. Naturally, Emma wanted to avoid the hospital, where she'd have to remove her shirt so her wound could be tended. Instead, she headed straight for the chaplain's cabin. Mrs. Butler, by now an expert nurse, cleaned and dressed the injured arm. "That ball nicked the flesh and went through," she said. "Nothing to worry about, my dear. You'll be fine."

Over a cup of coffee, Emma finally began to relax. "Thank you, Mrs. Butler," she sighed. "Guess I was mighty lucky."

The chaplain's wife shook her head anxiously. "You surely were," she said. "*This* time. . . ."

1 2

June 10, 1862

The colonel signed the furlough papers and handed them to Pvt. Thompson. "You've earned a good rest," he said. "Take two weeks; look after that arm of yours."

Thompson thanked him, saluted, and hurried to the hospital, where he packed a small knapsack. His arm was sore but healing well, and he looked forward to his holiday. A supply wagon train was just leaving for Fort Monroe and he hitched a ride as far as Williamsburg, a peninsula city occupied by the Union.

For a few days, as Pvt. Thompson, Emma explored the city, taking in the sights and sounds. But after months of danger and battle, civilian life seemed dull. She was soon bored and spent the rest of her leave doing volunteer nursing.

There were two main hospitals in Williamsburg,

filled with the sick and wounded. One hospital was for Union men, the other for Confederates. Emma saw no difference and divided her time equally between the two. As far as she was concerned, wounds were wounds and pain didn't play favorites. The war was a necessity, yes—but the price, the human price, was very high. Moving through the crowded wards, tending the rows of maimed and suffering men, she grieved for them all. But she kept in mind a prayer Maj. Butler had taught her. As the nurse worked, she repeated it to herself, gaining strength:

> *Grant us grace to share in others'*
> *woes . . . and when their dreams or*
> *hopes begin to fade . . . help our*
> *hearts to feel and our hands to aid. . . .*

By the end of the furlough, Emma's arm was healed, and she returned to camp fit and healthy— just in time for the final battle of Richmond. By now the Confederate armies had been greatly strengthened and had a new commander, Gen. Robert E. Lee. The fighting (later known as the Seven Days' Battles) raged back and forth, swirling around places called Mechanicsville, Frayser's Farm, Gaines's Mill, and Malvern Hill. In the end, the Union forces were completely stopped. McClellan's battered army had to withdraw to the west and dig in along the James River.

But Union troops were now needed elsewhere, and Frank Thompson's regiment—the Second Michigan—was sent to the Shenandoah Valley. Here they joined the Federal Army of Virginia under Gen. John Pope. At first the spy was alarmed, until she learned that Maj. and Mrs. Butler were being transferred, too. Hearing that, she breathed a sigh of relief.

At the new field hospital, Thompson's work went on as usual. But his reputation had followed him, and soon he was at headquarters again, serving as a special courier. The rebel commander facing them was the daring, brilliant officer, Gen. Thomas "Stonewall" Jackson. It was vital for Pope's aides to learn everything they could about Jackson's campaign plans, and before long, Pvt. Thompson was sent off again on spying missions.

Now that he was in a new zone, he felt it was safe to revive an old favorite. Several times in the hectic months that followed, he slipped behind enemy lines disguised as a small woolly-haired black man in ragged overalls—the amiable, good-natured Cuff.

To Emma Edmonds, Cuff had almost become a real person. "I truly admire the little fellow," she confided to Mrs. Butler, darkening her skin with solution and peering into the mirror. "He's a plucky one; got his share of grit." In the glass she saw Mrs. Butler grinning, realized what she'd said, and they both began to laugh.

In August, the two sides began skirmishing for a rail junction known as Orange Court House. Asked to find out more about the enemy's plans, Emma remembered the black women she'd seen at Richmond. She tinted her skin again, put on an old blouse, apron, and ragged skirt, and tied a bandanna around her head. She'd heard that a small group of contraband slaves, lonely and homesick, had asked to be returned to the Southern sector. Carrying a basket of laundry, she quietly joined this group and passed with them through the rebel pickets.

Emma spent the whole next day in the Confederate camp, washing and sewing for the rebels. By now she was an expert at keeping eyes and ears open, and picked up valuable data. Late that afternoon, she found herself alone in the wash tent. As she sponged and cleaned an officer's dress coat, a packet of official documents slipped from the inside pocket. The black woman was excited. She swooped on the papers and quickly hid them under her skirt.

Emma's heart was pounding. She'd made a great find—how could she get home quickly? Leaving the coat on its hanger, neatly cleaned, she hurried toward the slave quarters. Not far away a battle zone was being shelled. Emma had to act before the loss of the papers was discovered. So without stopping she slipped into this dangerous battlefield. Then she hid in the cellar of an abandoned farmhouse. She had no idea what would happen next. Would the rebels come after her? Would she be killed by a shell? She crouched in the dark cellar and waited.

All night, as she tried vainly to sleep, cannon shells and gunfire roared and crashed. Several times the old house shook with explosions. But somehow it remained standing. In the morning, Emma found that her luck had held. A troop of Federal cavalrymen overran the area, and Emma was free to come out of hiding.

With some difficulty, the strange black woman convinced the surprised troopers that she was a Union agent. Once she was cleared, she rushed to headquarters and turned over the precious papers.

Another time, a patrol captured two enemy horsemen from Kentucky. These Kentuckians, who had gone over to the rebel cause, all wore unique uniforms: pants and fringed jackets made of tan buckskin. Because of the color of their clothes, the men were called "butternuts." With the chaplain's help, Pvt. Thompson obtained one of these outfits and for several days roamed the enemy front as a Kentucky butternut, collecting more information.

For many months this pattern continued. Pvt. Thompson divided his time between hospital and headquarters, risking his life on spy assignments. Winter came, and with it, much cold and hardship for the troops. Twice, while riding Rebel on courier trips, Franklin suffered frostbitten feet. His ailments were very painful, but they never stopped him. He was doing what he wanted to do—playing a part in the great war effort—and even the imp voice was quiet.

At the end of the year, Pvt. Thompson and the Butlers were transferred again, this time to the Ninth Corps under Gen. Ambrose Burnside near Louisville, Kentucky. And while at this new post, Emma took on the toughest mission of her entire career.

February 17, 1863

If I had a cow that gave such milk,
I'd clothe her in the finest silk.
I'd feed her on the choicest hay,
And milk her forty times a day!
Ha ha ha! You and me!
Little brown jug, how I love thee!
Ha ha ha! You and me!
Little brown jug, how I love thee!

Couples skipped to this lively polka played by the Kentucky Militia Band. Candles glowed from chandeliers. Servants passed goblets of wine and punch to the guests. And in a side room, beautiful tables were heaped with sandwiches, pastries, and fruit.

The gala at the State House was a glittering event; all Louisville society was there. Most of the young men wore blue dress uniforms of the Union Army. The older ones looked dignified in frock coats and ruffled shirts. But it was the women who added color and elegance in their fine hoopskirts, elbow-length gloves, and gleaming jewels, with fans and dance cards dangling at their wrists.

From the festive look of things, it was hard to tell that Kentucky was in the middle of a grim war. At that very moment, rebel forces under Gen. John Morgan were carrying out guerrilla raids, and there was skirmishing near Louisville. But none of it seemed to bother the party-goers.

Two debutantes perched on gilded chairs were sipping punch and eyeing a slender young man who wandered about by himself. Unlike the others, Mr. Mayberry wasn't in uniform. His suit, well-cut and expensive, fit perfectly. He had blue eyes, dark wavy hair and a neat mustache, and moved with ease and confidence. The girls discussed him in whispers. Mr. Mayberry was a bit of a mystery; nobody knew much about him. One rumor had it that he was the heir of a wealthy Boston family who had been disowned for having Confederate sympathies. Another claimed the opposite: he was from a large Georgia plantation and had to leave home because he favored the Union cause.

Neither story was correct. The mysterious Mr. Mayberry was actually Emma on a new assignment, wearing another of her many faces.

Back at the Union camp, Gen. Hooker's aide had explained the situation. When the war began, three states—Maryland, Missouri, and Kentucky—were known as border states. Though they were slave-holding areas, they formed a kind of buffer zone between the North and the South. People in Kentucky were about evenly divided—they supported slavery but didn't want to secede and destroy the Union. It was a dilemma, and Kentucky tried to solve it by staying neutral.

Then in August of 1862, Gen. Kirby Smith invaded the state with a rebel army. Washington answered by sending Gen. Ulysses Grant and his troops to occupy the key town of Paducah. With war on its doorstep, neutrality for Kentucky was impossible, and the state finally went over to the Union side.

But wars aren't fought only on battlefields. Louisville became a center of undercover activity. Because of the divided feelings, there were many Southern sympathizers, as well as agents who fed valuable data to the rebel leaders in Richmond. Gen. Hooker wanted to stop all these leaks—and once again, Franklin Thompson was called in.

"This time," the aide said to Pvt. Thompson, "you'll work as a detective, not a spy. You won't be operating behind enemy lines, but in our own territory, among friends." The major tapped a street plan of Louisville on the map board. "This town is crawling with informers. Somehow the rebels know every blasted move we make. We know their main agent is feeding 'em facts *every day*. He's brilliant and very cagey. Your job, Thompson, is to find out who the devil he is."

The officer scribbled a name and address on a slip of paper and passed it to Thompson. "This is your contact in Louisville. He'll supply you with funds, clothes, and so on. We can't use him for this job because he's too well known there. What we need is a total stranger—a man with brains and backbone."

He stood up and held out his hand. "Keep your wits about you, Thompson. Get to know the pro-Southerners in Louisville. Take plenty of time, keep your eyes open—and don't get shot."

Franklin tackled the new job with confidence. In Louisville he met his secret contact, creating the new identity of "Charles Mayberry." Then he rented a room in a boarding house run by a woman said to have rebel sympathies. This had advantages for Mayberry: it tagged him as a possible Confederate supporter and gave him a chance to listen in on the other boarders.

Through his contact, he began to meet the city's important people and gradually to build an image.

He played his role carefully, tactfully; and by the time of the gala dance, Mr. Mayberry had gained a toehold in Louisville society. By then he also had a fairly good idea of the city's pro-Southern groups. But sympathy and political opinions didn't add up to treason. The chief Confederate agent—the man Mayberry was after—remained a total mystery.

At the State House dance, Charles strolled about in his fine suit, bowing graciously to his acquaintances. Now and then he casually stroked his mustache, pressing it gently to make sure the spirit gum would keep it in place.

Later he went into the refreshment room and helped himself to a sandwich. Nearby, at the end of the long table, he spotted P. N. Aylesworth, a short round man with auburn muttonchop whiskers and fat ruddy cheeks. Aylesworth, said to be very "pro-reb," didn't know it, but he was part of Mayberry's developing plan.

"Enjoying the party, Mayberry?"

"Indeed I am, sir," Charles replied, remembering to keep his voice in a low key. "Especially the food."

He gulped his sandwich hungrily and reached for another. Out of the corner of his eye he saw Aylesworth watching, and could guess what he was thinking: *These young blades . . . easy come, easy go . . . no idea how to handle their money . . . look at him, half starved. . . .*

"Mr. Aylesworth," Charles said between mouthfuls, "I have a bit of a problem. I wondered, sir, if I could stop by to see you tomorrow."

The fat man smiled. "Sure, Mayberry. Come 'round to the office first thing in the morning. We'll talk then."

Aylesworth was a wealthy dry goods merchant with a large, busy shop in Louisville. He also had contracts to supply Union regiments with blankets and uniforms. Early the following morning, Mr. Mayberry visited the shop and was directed to the owner's office in back. Aylesworth greeted him, then lit a cigar and leaned back at his rolltop desk.

Pretending embarrassment, Mayberry said, "Sir, I find myself a bit short of funds and needful of employment. I write a very fine hand and am good with sums. I . . . uh . . . thought, just possibly, there might be some opening for me here."

Aylesworth, his eyes keen, questioned the young man in detail about his background and opinions. To play safe, Mayberry mixed truth with fiction. He told Aylesworth he was born in Canada on a large, prosperous farm. After his education, he'd come to

America to make his way. He'd worked in various cities as a salesman and now, winding up in Louisville, was out of funds and in need of a job. He also let slip a hint that his war sympathies were very much with the South.

The merchant squinted and scratched his chin. It just so happened that his old bookkeeper was leaving and had to be replaced—as Mayberry already knew.

At last Aylesworth nodded. "I'll give you a chance, Mayberry—but mind you, it's only a trial. If you want to stay here, you'll have to prove yourself."

Mayberry thanked him gratefully and began to learn his new duties. For the next week, the young man worked very hard, always first at his desk in the morning and last to leave at night. The company's bills and ledgers were in a mess, and he was able to bring order out of the chaos, which pleased his busy employer. Aylesworth was so impressed with Mayberry that he even allowed him to handle an important sale—a big consignment of blankets—to a nearby army post. Riding on the wagon next to the driver, Mayberry worried that someone at the Union camp would recognize him and give the game away. But he needn't have fretted; with his fine mustache, dark civilian suit, and round bowler hat, he had no trouble passing. He left the shipment at the quartermaster depot, arranged for payments and receipts, then returned to Louisville.

After this success, Aylesworth began to rely heavily on him; he had a free run of the shop and stockrooms as well as the account books. Watching the people come and go, Charles also learned what he'd suspected: Aylesworth & Company was a clearing house for undercover rebel activities. He still couldn't put his finger on any hard evidence, but felt he was on the right track.

Aylesworth had one special friend—a tall, lanky, sour-looking man named Hall. He and the merchant had secret dealings; they would often closet themselves in the office with the door carefully closed and locked. Mayberry was anxious to eavesdrop on these little meetings, but knew it would be too risky to try.

Meanwhile time was passing. At night, lying awake on the lumpy, boarding house bed, Emma plagued herself with questions. Who was the gloomy Mr. Hall? Was he the man she was after? How could she find out? Where would she get the evidence she needed? Emma liked to make decisions and act on them. She hated the idea of personal failure, but she couldn't seem to break through the shell of secrecy.

Another frustrating week went by with no results. Then she came up with a wild plan. It was unusual—daring and dangerous—but it just might bring matters to a head.

It might also, if something went wrong, cost Charles Mayberry his life.

14

March 10, 1863

The next morning, Charles waited until the shop was quiet and there were no customers to attend to. He tapped gently on Aylesworth's door, popped his head in, and asked for a word in private.

Curious, the man waved him to a chair. "What can I do for you, Mayberry?"

The young man cleared his throat nervously. "I've . . . uh . . . come to a big decision, sir," he said in a low voice. "The . . . um . . . fact is, well, I've decided to join the Confederate army."

Aylesworth's bushy eyebrows shot up. "Bless my soul. Are you sure about this?"

Mayberry nodded. "Yes, sir. It . . . it was no hasty decision—I've been thinking about it a long time. You know that my sympathies have always been with the South; now I really want to do my part for the cause."

The merchant frowned. "War is no lark, boy. You realize you could be killed?"

Mayberry shook his head. "I'm prepared, Mr. Aylesworth. This is something I . . . I just have to do. I thought it out and have no choice, but I know it isn't easy to manage. I . . . uh . . . hoped, sir, maybe you'd be able to help me in some way."

Aylesworth lit a cigar, leaned back, and stared at the ceiling. "This comes as a surprise, Mayberry. We'll miss you in the shop. But I understand the need—yes, indeed." He went to the door and peeped out to make sure nobody was listening. Then he returned to the desk and lowered his voice. "If you're serious, I *can* help you. Tomorrow, leave the shop at your customary time. Come back shortly before nine o'clock. You'll find two horses out back, saddled and ready."

"Will you be my guide, sir?" Charles asked.

Aylesworth shook his head. "I believe you know my friend Mr. Hall? Well, he . . . uh . . . has certain dealings with the Confederacy. Has some, let us say, important documents to deliver. You can ride along with him. Hall has a secret route. From Louisville, you'll head south toward Garnettsville, and at one point a barge will ferry you across the river to the Southern lines." He patted Mayberry on the shoulder. "I admire your spirit, lad. Good luck with your plan—and not a word to anyone."

The young man's heart was racing; for the rest of the day, he had trouble concentrating on the books and ledgers of Aylesworth & Company. But quitting time came at last. Making sure he wasn't being followed, he hurried to meet his contact. When Mayberry explained what he'd done, the contact grinned with approval and told him to follow through carefully on the arrangements.

"Leave with Hall, just as planned," he said. "Somewhere on the Garnettsville road, you'll walk right into a Union ambush. Of course we'll have to arrest you both, to make it look good. But have no fear, Thompson. You've done splendidly—I believe we've got our man at last."

The following evening was moonless and overcast. Just before nine, Mayberry slipped into the yard behind the shop. Hall and Aylesworth were already there with the horses. Even in the darkness, Charles could sense the tall man eyeing him with suspicion.

"I don't like this, P. N.," he muttered angrily. "Who is this fellow, anyway?"

"No need to worry, Hall," the merchant said. "It's very safe; I'll vouch for the boy."

Finally the agent shrugged and swung up in the

saddle. As he did, Mayberry noticed the butt of a heavy Colt .44 pistol poking from Hall's belt. He mounted his own horse, praying that nothing would go wrong and that the planned ambush would work.

Together the riders turned south out of town and trotted along at a steady pace. Hall remained grim and silent; now and then he cast an evil sidelong glance at his young companion. Mayberry tried to make small talk, but finally gave up, and they rode for over an hour without speaking a word. The night was still, and Charles was beginning to get worried. Where were the Union troopers? Had something gone wrong with their timing? What would he do if the scheme failed?

Soon he could hear Hall muttering anxiously to himself. At any moment the man could pull his gun, shoot him, and dump his body in the river—and no one would be any the wiser. Mayberry's tension kept slowly building. Sweat trickled down his back. In the darkness Hall seemed to grow bigger and more menacing—a grim image foretelling doom. Charles fought to stay cool and composed. Under his breath he began to recite a beloved psalm to calm himself.

> *Yea, though I walk*
> *through the Valley*
> *of the Shadow of Death . . .*

A loud command tore through the silence. "Raise your hands, both of you!"

The spy almost whooped with relief as a squad of Union cavalrymen burst through the trees and surrounded them. Both travelers raised their hands as the captain in charge rode up and yanked the gun from Hall's belt.

"Tie 'em with their hands behind their backs," he barked.

Mayberry and Hall were quickly trussed, and in this ungainly manner, they turned off the road and headed toward a nearby Union encampment. They were now circled by the troopers and Hall made no attempt to escape. But Charles could still hear him muttering, cursing the Union, the entire government in Washington, and mostly his own bad luck.

Safe in camp, Hall was locked up and Mayberry was released with the thanks of the captain. Worn out, he found a quiet place to sleep.

The next day, he reported to Hooker's aide at headquarters. The officer beamed at him. "We caught him with the goods, Thompson. Those documents he had were secret Union plans he was taking to the rebels. In his papers we also found the names of two other agents in Louisville—a sutler and a traveling photographer. They've been nabbed, along with Aylesworth. A clean sweep. You couldn't have done better!"

Back at his own regiment, Pvt. Thompson was praised and congratulated. And on Gen. Hooker's orders, he was presented with yet another trophy: a handsome engraved sword taken from a Confederate major during the Battle of Fair Oaks, near Richmond.

Later, at the chaplain's quarters, Emma described the whole adventure to Mrs. Butler. She gave her the engraved sword for safekeeping, to be left with the rifle she'd brought back from Yorktown.

"Land sakes, all these trophies!" Mrs. Butler exclaimed. "I'm beginning to run out of room."

The two women laughed. Neither of them knew it, but this would be the last of Emma's hard-won souvenirs. More trouble was lying ahead for her, but it was of a different kind.

1 5

May 6, 1863

A few weeks after the Louisville episode, the regiment was transferred again, this time to Vicksburg and the army of Gen. Grant.

Vicksburg, on the east bank of the Mississippi River, was a Confederate rail center. If the Union could capture it, the Southern forces would be almost cut in two. But the city was well defended, guarded by river and swamplands on one side and steep craggy bluffs on the other.

The rebels' main defense was a system of trenches stretching for miles, from Haynes's Bluff to the Warrenton road. Since Grant's men far outnumbered the defenders, he tried to storm these trenches directly. But the rebels under Gen. John Pemberton, fighting skillfully, beat off every attack and left the Union with thousands of casualties. Finally Grant was forced to dig in, and a long siege began. Vicksburg was sealed off on the river side by Union warships; on the land side, Union artillery bombarded it with endless shells. Little by little, a noose of steel tightened around the besieged city. Later a Confederate soldier wrote home that "even a cat couldn't have crept out of Vicksburg without being discovered."

All this caused great suffering on both sides. The cannonading killed hundreds of soldiers and civilians inside the wrecked and starving city. Meanwhile rebel sharpshooters, hidden on the bluffs, picked off great numbers of Union men. At times the Federal troops had to crouch in trenches up to their knees in water, unable to raise their heads because of the hail of sniper bullets.

During these nightmarish weeks, Pvt. Thompson and the nurses worked without rest. The surgeons were completely exhausted. And Mrs. Butler, along with other officers' wives, came to the hospital daily to help tend the wounded.

Then Emma's luck—which up till then had been so good—suddenly ran out. For some time she had been feeling sick, but had been too busy to do anything about it. Her symptoms became worse, and at last she had to face the truth: she was suffering from malaria, or "swamp fever," as the soldiers called it.

Dr. Hodes and his assistants dosed Pvt. Thompson with quinine, but it did no good. The malaria was severe. One minute he burned with fever, the next he shook with a terrible chill. He could hardly sleep or eat, and found himself getting weaker by the day. Finally Thompson applied for leave, but gave no details, and his request was turned down. In this crisis, headquarters needed every single skilled nurse, and that was that.

Desperate, Emma turned to her trusted friend. "What should I do?" she wailed, sitting in Mrs. Butler's tent, shivering in an army blanket. "I can't just climb into a bed in the hospital. If I take my clothes off they'll know my secret—I'll be finished!"

Mrs. Butler paced the little tent unhappily. "I don't know what to say, my dear. You're very sick. You *have* to be hospitalized. Sakes, I'd nurse you here if I could, but there's no room. Besides, the major would learn the truth; he'd feel it his duty to report you to headquarters."

In tears, the women embraced each other. Then Emma trudged back to the hospital, feeling hopeless. She was ill and confused. Her world was splintering. Her imp voice was silent. For two years she'd posed as a man and had played the part well. To give it all up now, to be glaringly exposed, was a painful humiliation. Somehow, to Emma's fevered mind, it would shame her and make a joke of everything she'd tried to do.

She remembered feeling this same kind of deep

hopelessness when she was sixteen. Then, she'd solved the problem by running away. Now again, flight seemed the best way out—the only way out. Yes—she would leave quietly, get the help she needed, and come back to Vicksburg when she was stronger.

For Emma, to decide on something was to act on it. She left a brief note for Mrs. Butler explaining her plans and asking her to please look after Rebel. Then she packed her kit, took the money she'd saved, and slipped out of the nurses' quarters. Before dawn she hitched a ride out of camp on a drover's cart. Later, near Steele's Bayou, she took passage on a Mississippi riverboat and headed north to Cairo, Illinois.

Cairo was a bustling town, big enough to boast a hospital. Emma, weak and shaky, managed to buy a skirt, blouse, and bonnet. In a rented room, she changed from a Union soldier back to plain Miss Edmonds. Then she went to the hospital and signed herself in for treatment.

Emma remained in bed for several weeks, and with the proper food, rest, and medical care, gradually recovered. She followed the war news eagerly and learned that Vicksburg had surrendered. At the same time, an army under Gen. George Meade defeated Lee's forces in the Battle of Gettysburg. These two events helped the Union turn a corner; victory was still a distant dream, but was beginning to come closer.

Emma sensed the turn of the tide and, with her malaria under control, planned to rejoin her old outfit. Instead, she received another blow. Scanning the army bulletins in the window of the Cairo newspaper office, she saw that Pvt. Franklin Thompson of the Second Michigan was listed as AWOL—absent without leave! In the army's books, she had been branded a deserter!

For Emma Edmonds, a door suddenly slammed shut. Now there was no way she could take up her old work as a field nurse, courier, and Union spy. Pvt. Thompson was considered a deserter. He couldn't protest without an investigation in which the secret would surely come out.

For a time, Emma was heartsick. Then she reacted to this setback the way she always did: with action. Frank Thompson might be finished, but the war was still on, and there were many ways she could be useful. She sent word to Mrs. Butler telling her what had happened; then, with the last of her funds, bought a train ticket to Washington.

After her two years away, she found the capital more hectic and chaotic than ever. Wounded men were pouring in, and here, far from the fighting fronts, good nurses were badly needed. She found a place to live and went quickly to work in one of the base hospitals.

For the remainder of the war, Emma served as a nurse under her rightful name, tending and comforting the wounded. Now and then she would run into a trooper from Vicksburg or Yorktown and would ply him with questions about friends and acquaintances. She also followed in detail the battles of those final years. Chickamauga . . . Missionary Ridge . . . Spottsylvania . . . the Wilderness . . . Atlanta . . . Petersburg. Emma exulted in each Union victory and wept for the dead and dying of both sides.

Early in April of 1865, government troops finally occupied the battered rebel capital of Richmond. On the ninth of that same month, Gen. Lee surrendered the Confederate armies to Ulysses Grant— and at last the long ordeal was over.

Two days later, Abraham Lincoln made a speech from a window of the White House. The president, gaunt and weary, spoke of peace and honor, of charity and the healing of wounds. Among those in the huge crowd who cheered themselves hoarse was Emma Edmonds.

The Sunday after the South surrendered happened to be Easter, and Emma went to church. One of the songs that morning was an Easter hymn she'd always loved. As she sang with the others, she realized it could have been written for that very time in history:

> *The strife is o'er, the battle done,*
> *The victory of life is won,*
> *Our song of triumph has begun,*
> *. . . Alleluia!*

Looking back at the years of war, she thought of all the people she'd known and the roles she'd played. When she first enlisted in Michigan, it was a kind of lark. She'd had little idea what lay ahead. But she'd met all the challenges and done her best.

Emma's heart was full. Her beloved land was finally at peace. Now it was time for the healing.

16

What Happened After

What became of Emma Edmonds after the great Civil War ended? Government records and pension files offer some answers.

For a time, she kept on with her nursing work. She also sat down and wrote her memoirs, describing some of her adventures as Pvt. Thompson. In all, Emma spent two years as a man in the Union army and made eleven different trips behind rebel lines. On those spy missions she used various disguises, but her favorite was always the spunky little black slave named Cuff.

Her story came out soon after the end of hostilities. Titled *Nurse and Spy in the Union Army*, her book proved a big success and sold thousands of copies; Emma donated her share of the profits to U.S. war relief. The tale is hard to read because it is written in the fancy, flowery style popular in those days, but the reasons for what Emma Edmonds did are simple and clear. On the first page she says:

It was not my intention, or desire, to seek my own personal ease and comfort while so much sorrow and distress filled the land. But the great question to be decided was, what can *I* do? What part can *I* myself play in this great drama?

Morals in nineteenth-century America were prim and proper, and some people thought Emma's actions very shocking. But the publisher, W. S. Williams of Hartford, Connecticut, added a gallant note of defense:

Should any of her readers object to some of her disguises, it may be sufficient to remind them it was from the purest motives and most praiseworthy patriotism that she laid aside for a time her own costume and assumed that of the opposite sex, enduring hardships, suffering untold privations, and hazarding her life for her adopted country in its trying hour of need.

The little volume came out over 120 years ago. It has long since disappeared from our bookshelves and libraries, but surprisingly, a few ancient copies still exist. Their bindings are falling apart; the pages are torn and brown with age—yet Emma's adventures are as fresh and exciting as any tale of modern courage.

After finishing her writing, Emma grew homesick and went back to visit St. John, Canada. There she met Linus Seelye, an old friend from her childhood days. A romance soon began, and in 1867, Emma and Linus returned to the United States to be married in Cleveland, Ohio.

Linus was a mechanic and the Seelyes traveled a lot in connection with his work. They went from Ohio to Michigan to Illinois, finally settling in Fort Scott, Kansas. The couple had three sons, one of whom later joined the U.S. Army, "just like Mama did."

But Emma never fully recovered from her malaria, which she apparently first caught in the Chickahominy swamps. Her health slowly grew worse. She also began to brood about the shame of being branded as a deserter. Considering all she'd been through, she felt it a cruel, unfair label. She got in touch with officers from her old regiment and asked for their help. Encouraged by them, Emma petitioned the War Department for a full review of her case. She asked to have her military rights restored, including any back pay, plus an honorable discharge.

The matter was debated in Washington, D.C., and on July 5, 1884, a special act of Congress granted everything she asked for. Emma was awarded an honorable discharge, plus a bonus and a veteran's pension of twelve dollars per month.

By now Mrs. Seelye had made contact with a number of old army friends, including the Butlers. She kept in touch with them all and attended some of the regimental reunions. Most of her fellow troopers were, of course, amazed to learn that this plump, matronly lady in her fancy bonnet and long skirts was none other than their slim, cool-eyed war buddy, Frank Thompson!

In 1891, Emma's son Frederick was married and moved to the town of La Porte, Texas. Emma and Linus soon joined the young couple there. They liked the southern climate, and stayed in La Porte until Emma's death on September 5, 1898. Today her simple grave is in the military section of Washington Cemetery in Houston, Texas.

After the war, a group of Civil War veterans who had seen action in the Union forces formed a society called the Grand Army of the Republic. The GAR became powerful and important in American life, and had a huge enrollment of over four hundred thousand ex-soldiers. The only female member of this honored group was Emma Edmonds.

Other Reading

Would you like to read more about the Civil War and about the part brave women played in it? If so, here are other books that may be of special interest:

Barton, George. *World's Greatest Military Spies and Secret Service Agents*. Boston: Page Company, 1917.

Catton, Bruce. *The Civil War*. New York: American Heritage, 1985.

Dannett, Sylvia G. *Noble Women of the North*. New York: Thomas Yoseloff, 1959.

Dawson, Sarah M. *A Confederate Girl's Diary*. Bloomington: Indiana University Press, 1960.

Encyclopedia of the Civil War. New York: Harper & Row, 1986.

Fredericks, Pierce, ed. *The Civil War As They Knew It*. New York: Bantam Books, 1961.

Hoehling, Adolph A. *Women Who Spied*. New York: Dodd, Mead, 1967.

Kane, Harnett T. *Spies for the Blue and Gray*. Garden City, N.Y.: Hanover House, 1954.

Massey, Mary E. *Bonnet Brigades*. New York: Alfred A. Knopf, 1966.

Pratt, Fletcher, ed. *The Civil War in Pictures*. New York: Holt, 1955.

Pratt, Fletcher. *Ordeal by Fire*. New York: Harper & Row, 1966.

Ropes, Hannah Anderson. *Civil War Nurse*. Knoxville: University of Tennessee Press, 1980.

Shavin, Norman. *Illustrated Tales of the Civil War*. Atlanta: Capricorn Corp., 1983.

Stern, Philip Van Doren. *Secret Missions of the Civil War*. New York: Rand McNally & Company, 1959.

Have you read these ODYSSEY paperbacks?

ODYSSEY CLASSICS

L. M. Boston
THE CHILDREN OF GREEN KNOWE
TREASURE OF GREEN KNOWE
THE RIVER AT GREEN KNOWE
A STRANGER AT GREEN KNOWE
AN ENEMY AT GREEN KNOWE

Edward Eager
HALF MAGIC
KNIGHT'S CASTLE
MAGIC BY THE LAKE
MAGIC OR NOT?
SEVEN-DAY MAGIC
THE TIME GARDEN
THE WELL-WISHERS

Elizabeth Enright
GONE-AWAY LAKE
RETURN TO GONE-AWAY

Eleanor Estes
GINGER PYE
THE WITCH FAMILY

Carolyn Haywood
"B" IS FOR BETSY
BETSY AND BILLY
BACK TO SCHOOL WITH BETSY
BETSY AND THE BOYS

Anne Holm
NORTH TO FREEDOM

Carol Kendall
THE GAMMAGE CUP

Eleanor Frances Lattimore
LITTLE PEAR
LITTLE PEAR AND HIS FRIENDS

Milton Meltzer
UNDERGROUND MAN

Mary Norton
BED-KNOB AND BROOMSTICK
THE BORROWERS
THE BORROWERS AFIELD
THE BORROWERS AFLOAT
THE BORROWERS ALOFT
THE BORROWERS AVENGED

Carl Sandburg
PRAIRIE-TOWN BOY
ROOTABAGA STORIES, PART ONE
ROOTABAGA STORIES, PART TWO

Virginia Sorensen
MIRACLES ON MAPLE HILL

William O. Steele
THE BUFFALO KNIFE
FLAMING ARROWS
THE PERILOUS ROAD
WINTER DANGER

John R. Tunis
THE KID FROM TOMKINSVILLE
WORLD SERIES
KEYSTONE KIDS
ROOKIE OF THE YEAR
YEA! WILDCATS!
A CITY FOR LINCOLN
IRON DUKE
THE DUKE DECIDES
ALL-AMERICAN
CHAMPION'S CHOICE

Henry Winterfeld
CASTAWAYS IN LILLIPUT
DETECTIVES IN TOGAS
MYSTERY OF THE ROMAN RANSOM
TROUBLE AT TIMPETILL

Turn the page for more Odyssey titles and ordering information.

ODYSSEY BOOKS

Virginia Hamilton
A WHITE ROMANCE
JUSTICE AND HER BROTHERS
DUSTLAND
THE GATHERING

Paul Robert Walker
PRIDE OF PUERTO RICO

GREAT EPISODES

Kristiana Gregory
JENNY OF THE TETONS

Seymour Reit
BEHIND REBEL LINES